MEET ME at the BAMBOO TABLE

CHIN MUSIC
P R E S S

Copyright 2016
A.V. Crofts

Publisher: Chin Music Press
1501 Pike Place #329
Seattle, WA 98101

www.chinmusicpress.com

All rights reserved
ISBN: 978-1-63405-960-2

First [1] edition

Book design: Dan D Shafer, dandy-co.com
Cover photo: Josh Samson, samsonimages.com
Printing: Marquis in Canada, marquisbook.com

Library of Congress Cataloging-in-Publication Data

Names: Crofts, A. V. (Anita Verna), author.

Title: Meet me at the bamboo table : everyday meals everywhere / essays by A.V. Crofts.

Description: Seattle, WA : Chin Music Press, 2016.

Identifiers: LCCN 2016025995 (print)
LCCN 2016027989 (ebook)
ISBN 9781634059602 (paperback)
ISBN 9781634059619

Subjects: LCSH: Food habits.
Dinners and dining--Social aspects.
Crofts, A. V. (Anita Verna)—Travel.
Communication specialists—United States—Travel.
BISAC: TRAVEL / Essays & Travelogues.
LITERARY COLLECTIONS / Essays.
TRAVEL / Pictorials (see also PHOTOGRAPHY / Subjects & Themes / Regional).

Classification: LCC GT2850 .C75 2016 (print)
LCC GT2850 (ebook)
DDC 394.1/2--dc23

LC record available at https://lccn.loc.gov/2016025995

Printed in Canada

MEET ME *at the* BAMBOO TABLE

everyday meals everywhere

essays by
A.V. CROFTS

CHIN MUSIC PRESS • SEATTLE, WASHINGTON

For Mom, Dad, and Sarah

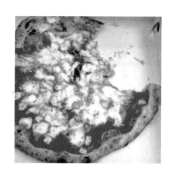

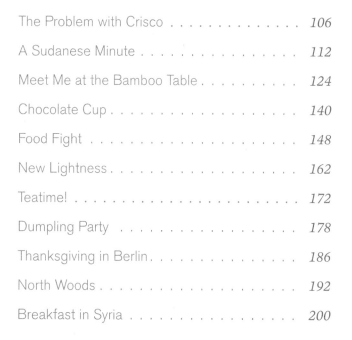

MY MEALS tell a story. Foods globetrot just like people. I once convinced a cashier at the first McDonald's in Beijing to sell me thirty frozen apple pies so my friends in southwest China could experience what was a rare treat from my childhood.

Lebanese falafel in the Ethiopian capital Addis Ababa. The *masala-málà* fusion of Chinese take-out in Mumbai. German *spätzle* beside bratwurst at a sauerkraut factory in Maine. Russian banter at an Uzbek restaurant in suburban Philadelphia. Meals anchor our experience of the world, wherever we are.

We eat to curb hunger. We feast to mark occasions. We consume for pure sustenance. Plans hatch over food and become banked in our memories. Meals mark our lives.

And, sometimes, they can change everything.

A.V. Crofts
Seattle, Washington

"Their lives spun off the tilting world like thread off a spindle,
 breakfast time, suppertime, lilac time, apple time."

– Marilynne Robinson, *Housekeeping*

China wove through my father's family history, but it was my mother who first got me to the Middle Kingdom. She was one of the two teachers who led a high school exchange program to Beijing, and I was one of a gaggle of students. The trip was ripe with family meaning. My mother and I crossed the Pacific Ocean by air as my great-grandfather had nearly a century earlier by sea when he set out from rural Ohio for China as a missionary.

Influenced by my time in Beijing, I chose to study Chinese when I headed off to college. This choice buried me under vocabulary flash cards and meant long afternoons glued to my seat in the language lab. I envied my classmates chattering blithely away in Romance languages after only a few months while I could hardly string a sentence together after two semesters of toil.

The best way to learn a language is a full linguistic baptism, so I went back and spent a semester studying in China. This time I arrived with a growing command of the language, unlike in high school, when I did not speak a word. I also had a greater command of myself. Humans are ever evolving, but my rate of self-discovery in my early twenties was exhausting. College provided a forum for reinvention, and the intimacy of meals during these six months dovetailed with my growing confidence. Food is fuel in more ways than one.

Thaw

NANJING is one of three Chinese cities referred to collectively as the "furnaces" because of their ferocious summer temperatures. Yet I spent much of my time there as an international student trying to chase away the cold.

It was January and, for the first time in my life, I was far more than a short distance from my family. They were thirteen time zones and three interminable flights away. Free alcohol flowed on these flights and the smoking section created a haze throughout the cabin, creating the feel of an eerily quiet airborne bar. Almost as soon as the final leg ended, I was determined to leave. The whole thing was clearly a grave mistake. The thought of being so far away from home was agonizing.

My first night in Nanjing I dreamed I was competing in a swim meet. During my race, a strong start had me way out ahead. Then on the last lap I gave up and blew my lead. I woke up just as I pulled myself out of the pool in the dream, dejected by my folly.

I threw off my covers, now wide awake. I got the message loud and clear. It might be the dead of winter, but it was time for me to come alive.

The single-paned windows in my Nanjing dorm room were no match for the winter air blasting in from the Gobi Desert. I wore gloves to warm my frozen fingers while scratching out my Chinese characters and leafing through my pocket dictionary. Clotheslines bisected the room and my laundry hung forlorn and damp for days. A photo of my girlfriend, Robin, was tacked to the recessed bookshelf above my bed. We met in Chinese class my sophomore year. She arrived in that first class a fountain of Chinese, fresh from an intensive summer program that left most of us sputtering in the dust. Chinese helped our friendship along as we began each weekday seated side by side in class. Time in class evolved into time laughing and talking outside of class, collaborating on crossword puzzles, swapping music, and me trying to keep up with her growing mastery of Chinese. Robin's smarts and quiet presence slowly grew to form my heart's fulcrum. She was not the first man or woman I had dated, but she was the first relationship that grew over time. In an ideal world, I would have been singing her praises from the rooftops. For now, though, she was my secret in plain sight.

My world was not ready. I was twenty years old and back in the closet. After being gobsmacked that anyone cared that I went with my girlfriend to the high school prom, I found college presented a clean slate. I was not the least bit ashamed of who I was—quite the opposite. I was pleased by my sensibilities: I liked men *and* women. However, I squirmed under the microscope of public opinion and now vigilantly protected my privacy. I accepted the sweet relief of anonymity that college, and now China, afforded. I bought a blue Mao jacket thick enough to hide in and a black Flying Pigeon bicycle as sturdy as a tank. Then off I went to find food.

There was no lack of possibilities. My exchange program provided a weekly meal stipend, and while modest by Western standards, it was a small fortune in China at that time. Besides, you never need a fortune to eat like royalty.

One early find was a noodle stand shoehorned into an alley near the campus gates. Square wood stools surrounded tables so small that they looked on loan from a nursery school. Cauldrons of hot water kept skeins of noodles boiling and acted as a heat source for hungry customers and cooks alike. Noodles were served swimming in a hearty broth with diced scallions, wilted greens, and a handful of shredded pickled vegetables strewed atop. The final preparation involved the cook cracking an egg straight into the bowl, where it poached on contact. Saucers of self-service chili pepper oil were on each table. This was the kind of heat I was seeking. I curled like a question mark over my large bowl of noodles. Each bite warmed me.

Meal expeditions included new classmates who quickly proved to be kindred spirits, though not yet the confidants they would become. We hailed from colleges and universities across the United States, joined by our study of Chinese. Amy had a wicked blond cowlick and wry sense of humor. Kind-eyed Don was a classical guitarist who often crooned to us in the evenings with his own whimsical songs. Adam was the brainiac with a razor wit. Tom was the sort who undertook a four-day train ride from Nanjing to western China with little more than eight large bottles of beer and the strength of his personality. We spent all our time together, bound by our shared adventure. When conversation turned to questions about sweethearts back home, I gave Robin and former girlfriends male first names that closely resembled their real names. And then changed the subject.

"Where should we eat?"

The answer was often the small eateries that were popular in the university neighborhood. Staples included *gōngbǎojīdīng*, a Sichuanese chicken dish that traced its history back to the Qing dynasty and arrived at our table as a magnificent plate of cubed chicken, red chili peppers, and peanuts. The *mápódòufu* pleasantly numbed our chapped lips with healthy doses of powdered Sichuan peppers over tofu. Pedestrian eggs and tomatoes twinned in *fānqiéjīdàn* to form a Chinese comfort dish with a hint of sugar. It is still my favorite dish when I cook Chinese food today.

Chinese dishes are designed to be eaten family style. Our camaraderie grew as we took turns deconstructing expressive dish names like *mǎyǐshàngshù* ("ants up a tree"). This exotic-sounding dish consisted of ground pork and translucent rice noodles tossed with red chili flakes—and it quickly became part of our rotation. The name actually comes from what it looks like when your chopsticks pull the noodles straight up from the serving dish or from your rice bowl to your mouth: a tree trunk flecked with tiny red dots. The poetic imagery packed in a dish name with only four characters is impressive. One month into my seven-month stay, half the shirts I owned had food stains down the front where an errant *jiǎozi* (pork dumpling) or *yúxiāngqiézi* (a brown sauce dish translated as "fish-fragrance eggplant") had tumbled into my lap. I chalked this up not to my chopstick skills but to a zeal for eating that sometimes placed speed ahead of sense.

Curiosity rewards the newcomer. As I grew bolder exploring the city, I discovered roasted sweet potato vendors at makeshift charcoal ovens converted from oil drums. They offered hot handheld meals for pennies. I fished out a few bills the size of Monopoly money and walked away with a blackened and blistered *kǎo hóngshǔ* that could feed three. It rested on two torn squares of yesterday's newspaper.

The warmth flooded my hands and hit my face as I squeezed the sweet potato apart to expose the deep orange-yellow flesh. In a season and a society with a bruise-colored palette, this splash of color dazzled. Chinese fashion still competed with boxy Mao suits of dark olive, battleship gray, or blue. Dull concrete apartment buildings were the same color as the frosty sky. Pelotons of black bikes spun their wheels in formation along major thoroughfares. The most colorful thing in Nanjing was the food.

The first bite of sweet potato required a calculation of hunger against heat—and hunger always won, leaving the roof of my mouth a victim of impatience. If I felt indulgent, I brought the sweet potato back to my room and dressed it in butter, using one of the foil pats I smuggled out of Nanjing's fanciest breakfast buffet in the pockets of my Mao jacket.

Food colored more than just the environment. It was often the first topic of conversation during my travels, as regions and cities in China had certain identities attached to distinct foods. At that time, China ate locally. This was not ideological but the reality of a nation playing catch-up on infrastructure. Food was not flown around the country. Greenhouses were not yet the norm. The weather dictated when crops were grown, and harvests were moved by manual labor from farms into cities. Nanjing was known for its strawberries, though once the season was over, the vendors hawking fruit piled high in their carts vanished.

Months and meals passed. China was in a drowsy state of coming-to after years behind a closed "bamboo curtain." The curtain was as much imposed as it was adopted. The anxiety in the United States about the rise of communism fueled dysfunctional diplomacy during the Cold War and an emphasis on containment. China at times closed its borders, deepening a sense of isolation from the outside world. Dependent at that time on its Soviet neighbor, China was impacted by political winds that continue to shift global patterns today. During my time in Nanjing, economic development was very much under way, and yet bicycles and horse-drawn carts ruled Nanjing streets. You could also still catch sight of bound feet on stooped neighborhood grannies. It was hard to imagine that ten years later urban economic development would render Nanjing unrecognizable. Internet connectivity and e-mail would become ubiquitous—no more waiting two weeks for a letter—and many of our restaurant haunts would be gone.

By the time my Nanjing semester came to an end, I had accumulated an impressive collection of letters and returned the favor in kind, mailing off page after page of my exploits on onionskin paper in airmail envelopes, stamps affixed with glue brushed on from a pot at the post office. I could throw back a flaming *báijiǔ* shot of high-octane Chinese grain alcohol, deftly manage slippery hard-boiled quail eggs with chopsticks, and make quick work of a giant bowl of pork dumplings. My letters documented the happiness that new friends and new places bring. They did not document how taxing it was not to be fully seen.

It would be a few years before I spoke freely of girlfriends with my friends from Nanjing, but I felt that possibility warming my core. Both China and I were growing into a new era of self-expression. I realized that instead of waiting for the world to catch up, I actually had to bring it along. Winter yielded to spring in Nanjing, and I, too, began to thaw.

航空
Par avion

THE CROFTS
1373 BUTTERNUT DRIVE
SOUTHAMPTON,
PA
18966
USA 美国

674100

If you want to
simply walk across
they will stop for you

In January 1983, my aunt gave birth to my first cousin in Paris, where my uncle was studying theater at the Sorbonne on a graduate scholarship. My mother needed no excuse to travel, but here was a great one. This decision was part of a longer game to inoculate her daughters with the travel bug. We boarded a flight to France the following summer—our first trip overseas. My father stayed behind to care for our suburban zoo, which at the time included a calico cat, two green parakeets, a growing family of Dutch rabbits, and an albino mouse.

I packed my cassette tapes and Sony Walkman in preparation for the trip. Early Bowie and B-52s. The Violent Femmes. I was fourteen. It was my second time on an airplane.

The Cost of a Cantaloupe

MY IMAGE OF PARIS was informed almost entirely by *Eloise in Paris*. Kay Thompson's uncanny ability to capture the voice of an impish six-year-old sophisticate and Hilary Knight's expressive illustrations created vivid pictures in my mind of sidewalk cafés, compact cars whizzing in circles on Paris roundabouts, and copious amounts of food and drink. Paris was a land of posh, indulgence, and bottles upon bottles of champagne. *La belle France* seemed worlds away from my suburban existence of carpools and casseroles. I was looking forward to it all. Especially the food.

I was taught French in elementary school, and I figured years of vocabulary call and response for vegetables, meats, and other foodstuffs would finally pay off. *Poulet! Pamplemousse! Haricots verts!* I was prepared to order chicken with a grapefruit and a side of green beans. In other words, I was in over my head upon arrival. The speed of native speakers rendered me mute. I was on the verbal equivalent of Eloise's Paris roundabouts.

But just because I could not muster the words did not mean I went hungry. I was smitten with buttery French croissants, my morning bowl of *chocolat chaud* cupped in two hands (*très magnifique*), and just about every morsel I ate in France. We made quick work of baguettes slathered with sweet cream butter. Cheese wrapped in waxed paper softened and did not last long in our care. I coveted the glazed fruit tarts whose *framboise* and *fraise* patterns resembled the stained glass rose windows of French cathedrals. Everything tasted richer. My days of Swiss Miss hot chocolate and margarine were *finis*. Champagne tastes became a badge of honor.

Excess was a departure from the family norm. My mother's family elevates frugality to an art form, believing thrift an attribute worthy of the highest respect. My grandparents lived through the Great Depression and my grandmother cooked for her family of five through the rebuilding years post-World War II. My mother was raised to prepare meals with leftovers in mind, reuse aluminum foil until it was near disintegration, and save money until she could afford a purchase. Carrying a balance on a line of credit was inconceivable.

While everyone practiced fiscal know-how, my grandmother, Gramanne to the grandkids, mastered it. She threw her car into neutral and coasted the final quarter mile home to save gas. She rolled a single pie dough serving thin enough for both a top and bottom crust. An envelope in her desk was filled with pieces of string, all too short to tie up a package, yet unthinkable to throw away.

All this being said, frugality must not be confused with austerity—now and again treating oneself is a must. While there were many meals during our week in Paris, one went down in family lore.

The restaurant for our splurge was teacup-sized, with linen tablecloths atop tables only inches from one another. I was used to a full arm's length from strangers, so dining in Paris initially clashed with my comfort zone, but I soon found that snug quarters added to the meal. No longer an invasion of my space, nearby diners became a stitched collection of appetites.

My family filled our seats with heady anticipation. Out came the menus, provided by our attentive waiter. Our eyes skimmed over the options. My grandmother's head snapped up.

"My menu has no prices!"

At that time, it was still customary in some restaurants to provide only the head of the household (eldest male) a menu with the itemized costs. My grandmother had a fit, demanding to see my grandfather's menu. The idea that she would consider ordering without factoring in price was unimaginable. My grandfather had a grace and a measured delivery that counterbalanced my fiercely intelligent and spirited grandmother. While he knew my grandmother would like nothing more than to study his menu and order something reasonable, he savored the freedom this might bring us all to follow our bliss.

He struck a deal with the table.

After reviewing his menu, my grandfather announced that there was one item we were not allowed to order: the South African lobster tail entrée. Given our family's ties to Maine, the thought of lobster in Paris was preposterous to begin with; however, my grandfather was not taking any chances.

We dove back into our menus.

When the waiter reappeared, Gramanne was still annoyed, but she placed her order. My sister and I compared notes and agreed that the cantaloupe appetizer sounded delicious as a summer starter. We each ordered one and spooned the sweet fruit into our mouths. I do not remember my main course, but the dessert was light-as-air *profiteroles* covered in warm chocolate sauce. I could have eaten a second or third plate as happily as I had the first. If this turns out to be the last meal I ever have in Paris, I will not complain. The pure pleasure remains.

Months after our return home and back around my grandparents' dining room table, my grandfather let us all in on a secret he had carried since the Paris meal. In his scan for high-ticket items, he had missed one doozy. The half cantaloupes my sister and I had ordered cost an outlandish eleven dollars each! This produced whoops of laughter and amazement in all of us. What my grandfather did not say that night in Paris says everything about his personality. Money is not the only thing that matters. That night, Grandpa Bill smiled and watched his two oldest granddaughters bask in the role of Eloise in Paris.

My first jobs after college were in the field of international education and student exchange. I felt a kinship with this cross-cultural clan because I was a former international student, and the number of invitations I received to visit students in their home countries grew every year. Eventually, the time came to start accepting these offers. With a newly minted graduate degree under my belt, I quit my job and bought an around-the-world plane ticket.

In the six months that followed, I spent only three weeks in hotels and the rest of the time as an honored houseguest. I was indebted to my students' eagerness to be cultural cushions in their home countries, as I had been for them in Seattle.

As I hammered out my itinerary, India topped my list. Most of my Indian students were in graduate programs, so they remained stateside for two years or more. This meant that acquaintances became friendships, often over meals. My Indian students missed their families' home cooking immensely. Nothing in Seattle came close. Given the chance to eat my way through India, I jumped and was not disappointed.

Mother India

SOME TRAVELERS collect sugar spoons or matchboxes. I have a knack for amassing surrogate mothers who make a mean fish curry or biryani.

In part, I have my name to thank. Quite a number of the half billion or so women in India answer to Anita. This resulted in many of the Indian graduate students at the University of Washington assuming that I was Indian when they saw my e-mail address. Imagine the surprise on their first day on campus when, muddled and tired-eyed from travel to Seattle, they discovered that their Indian Anita was as pale as rice *idli*.

After this initial confusion and, perhaps, disappointment, the students adapted. Part of me thought that these students harbored a hope that they could rub off on me and my inner Indian would be released. To a large extent, they did. When I made plans to travel to India, I found myself an ambassador of sorts on my own whistle-stop tour, delivering news to parents of their far-flung daughters and sons.

Indian mothers tend their children with dogged and loving attention, and I was a lucky proxy with the added advantage of being able to escape when affection approached suffocation levels. I absorbed their limitless ability to care for my every need, then regained my breath on the twelve-hour train ride to the next city. As the train disgorged me into a sea of weary travelers, a new Indian Mother of the Moment would magically appear, nearly levitating on the platform like a Hindu deity.

Each home provided a culinary immersion. I felt a twinge of guilt eating family dishes that my Indian friends had missed for years while they were in Seattle, so I decided the best way to mitigate said guilt was to eat with gusto. This was easy to do given the meals put before me. My friend Akhila went so far as to e-mail her mother ahead of my arrival with specific dishes to prepare for me, including *baghara baigan*, made by scoring plum-sized green eggplants and cooking them to velvety softness in a tangy tamarind spice sauce. Fortunately for me, her mother complied, amused by her daughter's long-distance catering instructions.

India is a kitchen crasher's dream. Fire-roasted *chapattis* steam your eyeglasses when you tear into these puffed bread pockets piping hot from the stove. Yoghurt *raita* helps cut the heat of fiery mango pickle. Fresh *poori* as thin as eggshells. The sweet heat of coconut chutney. I watched the Cricket World Cup while licking my Hyderabad Mother's silken eggplant dish from my fingers. My Chennai Mother introduced me to *dosas*, large rice and lentil pancakes that were rolled to the size of yoga mats and served with spiced potato filling and a side of *sambar*, a spicy vegetable soup made with chili peppers,

tomatoes, mustard seeds, and curry leaves. In Delhi I was served tomato and yellow lentil salad, a cool dish to combat the high heat. My Calcutta Mother showed me how to first warm uncooked rice in a puddle of *ghee*, or clarified butter, before adding seasoning and water for cooking. My Kerala Mother's fish curry was so good I would book a return trip just for one more taste. And my Mumbai Mother served spicy *chai* with breakfast and then walked me to the public bus, waving from the sidewalk after I boarded as though I was headed off to elementary school.

It was not lost on me that I was old enough to be a mother myself. All of my surrogate Indian Mothers regarded my backpack and unattached lifestyle with a blend of curiosity and concern. On one hand, I represented a culture that swallowed their children whole at the same time it offered great opportunity. My independent streak reinforced their perception that the United States prioritized individual freedom above all else, including the good sense to get married, settle down, and have children. Securing a spot studying at the University of Washington was a dream come true for their children and for them— but though they were thrilled by all that a successful degree would mean for their daughters or sons, I sensed also their hope for their children's return and their worry that their children might find themselves under the spell of a different country. On the other hand, my delight in their children and in their country endeared me to them. I did not feel judged. I felt doted on. And very well fed. If anything could lure their daughters or sons back to India after family, it would be the food.

I took note of the cooking utensils, spice combinations, grating techniques, and how central salt was to any savory dish. Everything was prepared by what appeared to be instinct, but was actually years of practice and recipes passed down through generations. Cups and teaspoons were handfuls and pinches. Like India itself, cooking required all your senses. Watching for onions to become translucent. Listening for the pop of mustard seeds. Tasting stew for salt with a dipped finger. I honed in with the same sensory intensity that I used while flying through rush-hour traffic on the back of a scooter in Chennai, handling bolts of raw silk in Delhi's silk market, and cupping my ear to hear the sound of my host's hand clap through the architectural design of a Mughal fort's tenth-century alarm system in Hyderabad. As my Chennai Mother said to me, "In this world I feel two eyes are not enough; you need a thousand."

While I have eaten many Indian meals in restaurants, nothing holds a ladle to those meals in the homes of my Indian Mothers. By feeding me, they fed the empty spaces their daughters and sons left behind, and the hope that the next mouth they fed from Seattle would belong to one of their own.

As part of my work with the University of Washington Department of Global Health, in 2010 I joined a university partnership to deliver trainings in Namibia. This involved long-haul trips from Seattle to Namibia's capital, Windhoek.

Namibia is the second-least densely populated country in the world. Driving across the country affords majestic views of towering white clouds against sky, a stretched horizon, and hardly a sign of human habitation. Its northern shoreline includes the "Skeleton Coast," a treacherous stretch named for the many shipwrecks and whale bones that washed to shore during the height of the whaling industry. My first time walking the beach in the town of Swakopmund, I half expected a pirate ship to bob into sight out of the salty shroud.

Namibia is a young country politically and demographically, even though the land itself is ancient. The country gained independence from South Africa in 1990, ending a long era of occupation that began with colonial Germany in 1884. While the Germans ceded their claim to Namibia after World War I, the painful imprint of enforced segregation, relocation, and the subjugation of indigenous tribes still echoed in Namibian society when I visited. This was my first time in an African country with a substantial white population, and the experience challenged my perceptions of the continent.

A Common Language
of Meat

EACH TIME I LANDED at the Windhoek International Airport, the view from the tarmac was glaringly blue sky and vast rust-colored plains in all directions. Instead of feeling dwarfed by Namibia's wide-open spaces, I saw such expansiveness as freeing.

Though the airport was a single terminal, acres of parking lots abutted the building. Colorful tents pulled tight atop poles shaded shiny new cars. While some were for hire, many appeared to belong to passengers; this was one of my first indications of the household income spread in Namibia. No matter how many times I visit Africa, I have to check my assumptions of what it means to be Namibian or Ethiopian or Egyptian. The West tends to view the continent as a monolithic entity, defining it by its most intractable issues instead of its astonishing diversity. Reality is often found in the contrasts. Single-family farms dotted the Namibian landscape approaching the capital city, yet in the space of a mile, unsettled terrain became an urban center full of cosmopolitan white and black Africans shopping at malls and working in shimmering glass skyscrapers. There were ATMs on every corner.

Similarities are also revealing. As my Namibian colleague once said to me, "Meat is the language that Namibians have in common." In a country of deep divides—Namibia has one of the widest gaps between rich and poor on the planet—meat is something most Namibians can agree on.

Meat starred in nearly every one of my meals, from grand buffets to casual street food. Given Namibia's fresh fruit and grains, a visiting vegetarian would hardly starve; however, they would be viewed with a skepticism bordering on incredulity. It was not unusual for my hotel breakfast spreads to include plates of cold cuts followed by four or more chafing dishes of hot sausages and slabs of bacon. I once ordered a beef entrée for lunch and was served a plate with not one but two cartoonishly large steaks. Another time, I needed both hands to heft a foot-long skewer of springbok kebob. One evening after an outdoor barbecue, or *braai*, I sat in a circle with my Namibian and American colleagues, full of pork ribs, oryx fillets, and chicken wings, and told jokes as the moon rose.

African tribes air-dried meat well before any Europeans set foot on the continent, yet early Dutch settlers to South Africa introduced the practice of curing with vinegar. It then migrated north to Namibia and stuck. One particular meat preparation, *biltong*, involves air-drying small pieces of meat into lengths or bites of jerky. *Biltong* involves a vinegar wash and spice rub, and the arid climate in Namibia is ideal for its production, especially in the dry winter months. Banish all thoughts of shoe leather—much of Namibian *biltong* maintains a moist quality that makes it all the more addictive. *Biltong* shops in Namibia reminded me of candy stores: they featured bins of various preparations, spices, and meats in display cases with helpful staff who fill paper bags at your request. The comparison is apt, as the best *biltong* I have eaten could be described as meat candy.

One sun-saturated afternoon I visited Katutura, a Windhoek neighborhood where indigenous Namibians were forcibly resettled during South Africa's rule and the introduction of apartheid. I was meat-obsessed and wanted to learn more. Israel Hukura, a member of the Herero tribe, who are historically cattle herders, accompanied me. Israel had a youthful face with just a hint of white-flecked stubble that placed him closer to middle age. He wore an outback hat cinched at the chin and a gold wedding band as thin as a pin. Israel put it to me plainly: "No meat? No meal."

Israel explained that in the Otjiherero language, Katutura means "the place we do not want to live." Not only did Katutura residents face resettlement and the loss of prime land, they also had to pay for rent (blacks could not own property under apartheid), utilities, and the public bus system that was introduced to bring blacks to the city center to work. In the fifty years since Katutura's establishment, its infrastructure had grown, as had the footprint of Windhoek itself. A pronounced disparity existed between the broad boulevards and high-rise office buildings of the shopping district in downtown Windhoek and the maze of residential streets and homes of Katutura. At times I felt like I was in two countries that shared a city.

As we arrived on the outskirts of Katutura, Israel told me that the Windhoek city center did not feel like Africa to him. His observation mirrored my own impression and presented a philosophical conundrum hard for me to solve. While I worked to remind myself of the breadth encompassed by the word "African," this native Namibian saw parts of his own country as unrepresentative. In Israel's mind, Katutura was a more accurate African experience. He told me that over a decade before, a friend of his had the idea to bring tourists to Katutura. Tours existed at well-known downtown Windhoek sites such as Christ Church and Parliament Gardens, so why not create tours that showed tourists a vibrant yet rarely visited section of the city? People said he was nuts: there was too much crime and it was too dirty, too loud. Ignoring the naysayers, he went ahead and promoted Katutura tours. They were a resounding hit.

However, tourism of this kind has its detractors well beyond Namibia. Allowing privileged tourists to parachute into towns or neighborhoods of scarcity, take hundreds of photos with expensive cameras, and then return to their lives of relative plenty understandably rankles many who live in these communities. Tourism dollars are nice, but pride has no price for some. I wrestled with this ethical dilemma and my outsider status experiencing insider access that I did nothing to earn. Even well-intentioned inquiry can sometimes leave a bad aftertaste.

Our destination that day was Oshetu Market. The market acted like a town square for the neighborhood. While vendors hawked everything from hops to make beer, to sorghum, wheat, and millet powder, what caught my attention were the *outete* grills ("pieces of meat") just beyond the butcher stalls in the market. A string of five wood-fueled cement-block grills sat side by side, each a bit above waist height. The grillers retrieved fresh bite-sized beef from the butchers behind them, which they seared and sold by the cube. Customers congregated in front, plucking the meat piping hot off the grill and dipping it in salt and chili pepper, or taking their snack away in a newspaper cone.

By the time I tried my first *outete*, I had tasted many meat dishes in Namibia. None could beat the flavor and freshness of this street food. It was a struggle not to shovel the ferociously hot, addictively spiced meat into my mouth. Fast fingers were all I needed for this meal. When we finished, Israel dropped me back at my downtown hotel, both of us feeling like visitors.

Pickles

Travel begs comparisons. We navigate new terrain by juxtaposing it against what we know. Tastes that resonate, even when dressed up in different outfits, comfort us with familiarity amidst the unfamiliar.

Pickles pop up just about everywhere. Their universality makes them culinary touchstones that bridge cultures and translate across tastes. Ultimately, it is our shared appetites that bind us. Humble pickles, thankfully, are always ready to serve.

Sidekick

I HEREBY LODGE a formal complaint against the negative connotations of the phrase "in a pickle," which paints a picture of discombobulated vegetables swimming in brine. What could possibly be bad about a pickle?

I am talking about the vinegary wince and crunch of a do-not-mess-with-me dill, the savory tones of a Japanese *tsukemono*, or Indian *aam ka achaar*, a spicy mango pickle whose heat I tame with a yogurt chaser. Pickling goes back centuries. Spin a globe and no matter where it stops, there is likely pickling of some kind to sample. What started as a necessity has lasted because fermentation is as delicious as it is practical.

Pickling is preservation. It is the blend of a few ingredients—salt, spices, vinegar, and a vegetable—and the promise of future satisfaction. Pickles are the opposite of instant gratification. But the time required is primarily shelf time, not preparation.

These potent sidekicks cheer the most lackluster main dish. They are the chartreuse canoe next to a BLT with a side of fries. The daikon radish's yellow half-moon smile alongside hand-pressed Japanese *onigiri*, still warm to the touch. Variegated coins on cheeseburgers. A forest of spicy green beans sharing a mason jar with dill flowers, chili peppers, and cloves of garlic.

The superb pickle is too often relegated to second class. It is called a condiment instead of revered as an exercise in patience and the value of foresight. A pickle is the ultimate demonstration of optimism. Pickling is a way of saying "I will enjoy you another day."

There was a Jewish delicatessen not far from my childhood house in suburban Philadelphia. My father was partial to their rye bread—unsliced—and the staff behind the meat and cheese case always announced his arrival with a booming "Hey, Pro-fess-ah!" then reached for a fresh loaf, already sure of his order. I was taken with the barrel of kosher pickles in front of the case, possibly because at the time the barrel and I were about the same height. Stout gherkins floated amidst peppercorns in a vinegar bath under a Plexiglas top. Tongs were available, as well as waxed paper bags that slowly decomposed around the wet pickle—all the more reason to eat it promptly.

It was not uncommon during my meals in China to begin with *pàocài*, pickled vegetables often showcased in large glass apothecary jars. Cleavered radishes and turnips were set in spices and vinegar to pickle, with whole chili peppers sometimes turning the bobbing contents frosting pink. My first visit to a

Korean restaurant found me stuffed by the time my main course arrived; I had devoured the *banchan*, center-stage starter bowls of *kimchi* and other pickled vegetables. Korea has a subterranean collection of clay *kimchi* pots that use natural temperature regulation and the seasons to achieve effervescence. Japanese restaurants offer pickle plates so artistic it is as if they are composed of vegetable gemstones: wee glassy onions, eggplant tidbits, and a collection of tiny cauliflower trees. Not all Japanese pickles conform to such stylish ways. My friend Yuko gave me my own plastic pickle press so I could replicate the chopped cucumber pickles she served me at her home. I have peered into the bottom of a small wooden bucket as my friend Yoshi used long chopsticks to excavate *nasu no misozuke*, preserved pieces of eggplant buried for days in miso. While the salt-shriveled specimens were not much to look at, they tasted beautiful.

Today, on the lowest shelf of my fridge sits a small canning jar of preserved lemons. Lemons, salt, and time are the only ingredients. The bright peels soften under the salt slurry to a tender version of their rigid selves. And it is the peel that you want. A simple plate of pasta achieves rock star recognition with a half teaspoon of this minced preserved lemon. It has saved my dinner more than once.

A number of containers of pickled limes have eluded customs officers over the years, swaddled in suitcases as my friends made their way back to the United States. Edible contraband for some. Edible memories for others. Preserved.

PICTURESQUE

ESTONIA

The Seattle Public Library hosts a yearly book sale to trim their holdings and raise funds to purchase new titles. Among dog-eared copies of bestsellers, patient bibliophiles like me unearth treasures.

Such it was the year I spotted a battered copy of *Picturesque Estonia*, a collection of black-and-white photographs published in 1950. Estonia is the northernmost country in the Baltic states, situated as if blowing a kiss northward across the Gulf of Finland to its Nordic neighbors. My new find featured Tallinn, Estonia's capital city and the location where I toasted my thirtieth birthday. When I opened the book to a photograph of the Town Hall Square in Tallinn's historic center, I was struck by how little the view had changed in fifty years.

Life's milestones are often marked by meals, and while I think back on the company, the ambiance, and the dinnerware, strangely for me, what exactly I ate for my birthday is gone, just as fullness fades and becomes hunger again. Meals are much more than simply what is eaten. The who, the where, and the why all contribute to the memory.

Independence

ESTONIA WAS BOTH YOUNG AND OLD at the turn of this century, and I felt the same way. My friend Amy was in Estonia as a Peace Corps Volunteer, so I had an open invitation to visit. I wanted to see what the country looked like almost a decade into independence from the former Soviet Union. Like Estonia, I valued the autonomy that independence brings; however, like Estonia, I still moved through phases of adulthood. Thirty was a threshold to even greater independence.

My first moments in Estonia provided a glimpse of things to come: the public e-mail stations for passengers in the Tallinn airport terminals stunned me. Their screens encased in blond wood and glass were the first I had ever seen. Three days later, as Amy and I coaxed our sewing machine-engine rental car across the countryside on the Estonian island of Saaremaa, a farmer stood ankle-deep in a freshly plowed field talking on his cell phone. I would not own one for another three years. Estonia was like being in the future.

Other days, it felt like time travel to the past. Rumor had it that the KGB set up offices in valuable Tallinn real estate on the Town Hall Square during the Russian annexation in the 1950s. The square's historic architecture and medieval city walls were relatively untouched during that time, surviving neglect and mounting debt as the Soviet Union folded. While sibling cities like Vilnius in Lithuania saw their historic city walls succumb to new construction in the nineteenth century, a decade into independence the center of Tallinn was still remarkably preserved. That said, a short walk from Tallinn's core landed me in residential neighborhoods with uninspired concrete high-rises emblematic of the former Soviet system that placed function ahead of form.

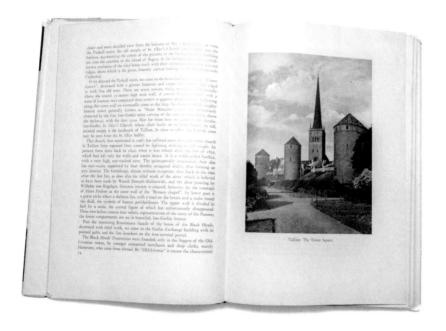

One interpretation is that Estonians were happy to wind back the clock, as if the preservation of the center square helped them shed the memory of their most recent uninvited master and reestablish their sovereignty. More likely, the country was investing elsewhere in infrastructure (the airport, for instance) and saw benefits in keeping the historic center relatively intact. Architecture can be a form of national storytelling, and Estonia definitely had a story to tell. This was evidenced by the decision to maintain a center square free of billboards and fast-food chains, and also by the restaurant Olde Hansa, which served Estonian recipes on hand-turned wooden plates accompanied by drinks in blown glasses. These glasses were heavy in the hands and dense with bubbles trapped when the molten glass cooled. What could have felt kitsch instead felt sacred.

I kicked off my thirties at Olde Hansa on a day that remained twilight for all but a few hours when the sun dipped ever so briefly below the horizon. Poring over the menu, I thought it fitting that Estonians positioned a restaurant of such national pride and culinary history in what had been the shadow of Moscow rule.

Though I kept travel journals at the time, this night remained undocumented but not unmarked. I bought a pair of those green glasses and they live in my cupboard to this day. Back then, I knew I wanted something tangible and useful that would connect me to the trip once I was home. I was captivated with how solid something as fragile as glass could feel. This dichotomy also reflected my own solidifying self. Within two years I would shift careers and put down even deeper roots in Seattle. The heft of the glasses weights the delicate nature of memory. Each time I use them, I am reminded of how travel yields a kaleido-scope of experiences that we can, sometimes, if lucky, hold tight in our hands.

I was on my fifth passport before I first stepped foot in Alabama. In my imagination, Alabama meant brackish tributaries leading to the Gulf of Mexico and farmland awash with cotton fields, a lasting backdrop to the bitter history of slavery. The South felt like a foreign country to me.

Overseas travel confers the role of outsider that lets you view a place with a detachment that can curb assumptions. Not so for me and Alabama. Alabamians and I share a national identity, a history, and a responsibility to learn from this history and each other. This trip offered me a chance to survey my own backyard in the same spirit with which I took on the world.

Because I am the daughter of a historian who writes about the Civil War, my childhood breakfasts regularly included a taste my father acquired during research trips south of the Mason-Dixon line: fried eggs over grits and shredded cheese. My father's collection of books about the American South dominated the shelves of our home, but I am unmistakably a Yankee. The opportunity to travel to Alabama arrived in the form of a civil rights pilgrimage sponsored by the University of Washington Department of Communication. Students, faculty, staff, and community members traveled to four Southern states to hear history from those who lived it and visit sites that memorialized those who died in the ongoing struggle for racial equality.

The trip also provided a chance to spend time with my father—on a road trip with thirty-eight others. My father came of intellectual age during the civil rights movement and it affected his life work in significant ways. I came of age a hundred years after the Civil War, in a country still wrestling with the legacy of racism. Over nine days, our group visited numerous civil rights milestones. Each site triggered a reckoning with the past.

A More Perfect Union

THE SOUTH PROVIDES many extremes—one of which is temperature. It was October and the thermometer cracked ninety degrees at noon in Selma, Alabama. My father and I sought shade wherever we could find it. Hours later, in nearby Marion, we shivered in the air-conditioned Judson College auditorium.

We were on the move most days from sunup to sundown, with little time to linger over meals. Breakfasts were hastily taken in the dual-purpose lobbies of budget hotels, and the only inkling that we were in the South was the packets of instant grits alongside instant oatmeal. We ate in motion. Lunches were take-out sandwiches in Styrofoam clamshells with sides of potato chips. Given our jammed schedule, dinners were take-out fried chicken, pasta and salad buffets, or pizza. The pilgrimage had not been one of culinary fireworks.

Food does more than just curb hunger; it reveals the narrative of culture. It is about people and their sense of place. You can cover a thousand miles but not know people until you have eaten their food. All my hope rested in the meal that the Marion community was preparing for the final night of our trip—word was that they were pulling out all the stops. I soon learned that this meant local matriarch Mrs. Viola Wright had been very busy in her kitchen.

After a mesmerizing performance in the frigid auditorium, we entered a private dining room with round tables set with linen tablecloths. Mrs. Wright stood tall behind a chafing dish of collard greens that shone emerald. Two trays flanked the greens, one filled with cornmeal-battered catfish, the other stacked with cornbread. Macaroni and cheese with extra melted cheese on top completed the meal. The latticed peach cobbler still bubbled from the oven.

This was the meal I had been waiting for.

I approached the serving table and introduced myself. Offering my hand to Mrs. Wright, I asked if she was in part to thank for the meal. She nodded with a shy smile.

"Those collards?" Yes.

"That catfish?" Yes.

"This cornbread?" Yes.

"The cobbler?!" Oh, yes.

Her smile grew wider with each query. It became clear that the only thing Mrs. Wright had not prepared was the macaroni and cheese. She was almost single-handedly responsible for this meal that would feed nearly sixty. Many communities have gatherings, such as potluck suppers or potlatches, where tables groan under the weight of meals cooked by many. But only the luckiest have the equivalent of Mrs. Wright—cooks with the wizardry to feed a crowd that would paralyze most of us. I sensed from her composure that Mrs. Wright saw her efforts as service to a higher set of ideals: generosity, stewardship, and faith. While we were strangers to Marion, and I was a stranger to Mrs. Wright, both treated my group as valued guests at tables set for a feast.

History is not just read. It is tasted.

And taste it we did. Served on dusty rose-colored Judson College dinnerware and accompanied by sweet tea in dew-beaded glasses, my meal was a still life of Southern culinary hospitality. I scanned the room and saw my father on the far side seated between two students, eating a generous helping of macaroni and cheese.

That night at Judson College, history was also heard. After we cleaned our plates, a microphone moved from table to table as our Marion hosts told first-hand stories of the modern civil rights movement. Some recalled the 1965 march from Selma to Montgomery in support of voter registration, an event that broadcast police brutality into households across the United States, cata-lyzing public outcry and a path to the Voting Rights Act later that year.

When the microphone found Mrs. Wright, we discovered that her singing was just as impressive as her cooking. Music was a central feature of the civil rights movement. It swelled collective momentum toward acts of nonviolent civil disobedience and lifted flagging spirits in the face of physical danger. Songs that bolstered communities in churches and cotton fields became anthems for change.

With no accompaniment she began to sing "By the Grace of My Lord, I've Come a Long Way," elongating each syllable as if still in mourning for the pain of the past.

Could have been dead
Sleeping in my grave
By the grace of the Lord
We've come a long, long way
People talk about us
Just as much as they please
But the more they talk
I'm staying on my bended knees
By the grace of the Lord
I've come a long, long way

We are half a century beyond the events in Selma, Marion, and Montgomery, but the struggle for an equitable and just society continues. That night in Marion, Mrs. Wright satisfied my appetite while feeding my hunger for a more perfect union.

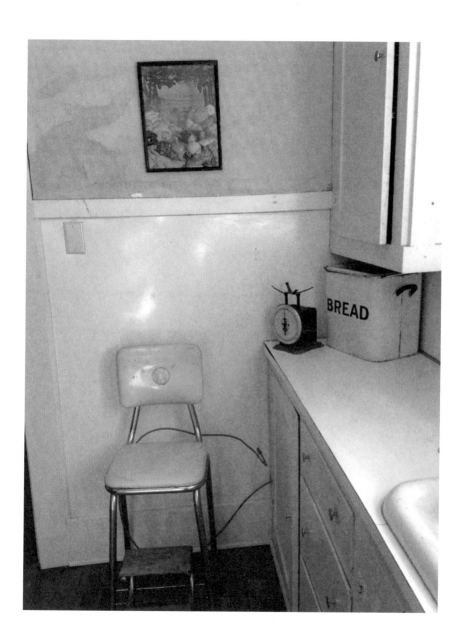

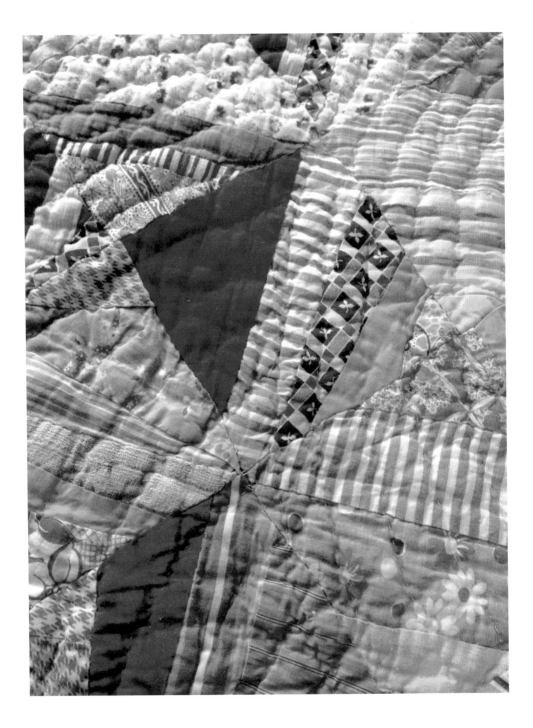

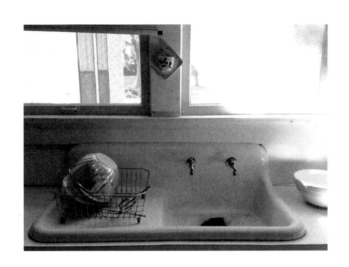

In 2002, I felt my next career move coming. My work with FIUTS, the Foundation for International Understanding Through Students at the University of Washington, had been tremendous. I was only months from finishing a graduate degree in public administration and on the hunt to purchase my first house. Eight years in Seattle was enough time to make the city mine but also long enough that I pined to travel. I am a hybrid, a homebody with wanderlust.

By the end of the year, I had that graduate degree and a house. I had given notice at my job. Renters were lined up, I had bought an around-the-world ticket, and the trusty backpack that traveled with me through my twenties was now strapped to my back. With an international constellation of friends to see, my vision for the trip was a sequence of dinner parties that kicked off in New Zealand, where, thanks to the International Date Line, I could ring in the new year before most of the rest of the world.

Intermission

ONE DECEMBER I escaped Seattle's winter darkness and landed in Auckland after the longest flight of my life, squinting into the summer sunshine. A short domestic flight later, I arrived in Wellington, a city folded inside the snail-curl of a peninsula facing the sea.

Sophie and Pete, her Kiwi husband, were my welcome team. Sophie and I became fast friends in China the year after we graduated college, brought together at first by a mutual friend, then by fate when she locked herself out of her apartment and I was the only one in the guesthouse during the Christmas holiday who could help. I successfully broke in by performing a Spider-Woman feat of entry via an outdoor window and immediately earned Sophie's respect and love forevermore. She and Pete met shortly after while working in Cambodia. They fell for each other's nimble minds and senses of humor, but if you pushed Sophie, she would also include Pete's mad cooking skills. He can dispense cookery wisdom as if rattling off a grocery list. Pete puts meals on the table that make a weekday supper taste like a state dinner.

Pete arranged for me to stay in his brother's Victorian five-bedroom house. It had wide staircases, wainscoting, and front and back gardens. A wraparound porch snaked with clematis opened into the kitchen, which led into the dining room and palatial sitting rooms full of overstuffed couches and curios. Elaborate model wooden ships were docked on mantelpieces. Paper-mache masks hung next to vintage photos of the Statue of Liberty. My bedroom was filled with the smell of cut white lilies set on my bureau in a vase and faced a patio profuse with ferns and blue-glazed urns. Each main door had brass lion-head knockers, and chandeliers hung from downstairs ceilings. I wandered from room to room as if the house were a museum. Nothing matched, yet everything fit perfectly. It was only the first stop on my nine-month journey and I never wanted to leave.

The temptation to shred my ticket increased as I began to eat my way through New Zealand. Summer allows a country to show off a bit. We went strawberry picking, barbecued on the beach, and vineyard-hopped on the south island. Savory hand pies charmed me—you could count on rest stops and gas stations to have a small case of them on offer. One night I tugged fresh lemons from trees at a backyard dinner. Nature presented jaw-dropping scenery and the outdoors invigorated my taste buds. I remember a Wellington brunch at The Chocolate Fish, a seaside café. The sun was climing overhead and our food was on its way. Laughter reigned as tea arrived in a stainless-steel pot, accompanied by a small glass bottle of milk that looked straight out of a traveling medicine show. All things felt possible.

Instead of feeling uplifted, though, I was daunted by the adventure before me. This trip was an intermission between acts. My years between college and this moment were focused on the adornments of adulthood: a good job, health insurance, a house, a retirement plan. At the end of the day, however, I was alone. The idea of marriage held appeal yet felt abstract; the concept was theoretically wonderful but hard to imagine for myself. I relished my independence and broke off relationships when the choice to move toward an official we versus me loomed and forced my hand. The years before this trip were full of weddings—in one twelve-month stretch I attended eight in as many states. One of them was Sophie and Pete's. My decision to gallivant on my own brought my chosen singlehood into sharp relief. Paradoxically, during the next nine months away from my Seattle home, I fixated on the trappings of domesticity I had traded for the solitude of independent travel.

Before leaving on my trip, I thought I was chasing the sun: I started with barbecues in New Zealand and ended five months later with a summer in Maine before returning to Seattle in September. In truth, I was chasing a future version of myself. No itinerary could quell my restlessness. It ran deeper, and the only cure was my own company.

I studied Russian and Chinese in college, which some teased me was preparation for a career in espionage. The summer before my senior year, my mother suggested that we travel to the Soviet Union while I still had a good enough grasp of the language to chat up the locals and stay out of trouble. Mom had fostered my adventuresome travel heart from the start. I was finishing up six months of study in China at the time, so she proposed joining me in Beijing for a journey on the fabled Trans-Siberian Railway, which threaded through northern China, the entirety of Mongolia, and a broad swath of Russia.

Mom sweetened the pot by arranging our housing through a travel agency that specialized in homestays, so we had the advantage of hosts in each place we visited. And, in the ultimate gesture of maternal affection, she booked us a private double-sleeper with an attached bath. Given that I had spent much of my time in China riding long-distance trains in cattle-car conditions—one torturous overnight I slept in a dining car's empty cabbage bin—this sounded luxurious. I fantasized about compartments with cut crystal light fixtures and plush velvet-covered seats to hold worldly passengers with gold pocket watches and furs. Whooshes of steam and a mournful whistle would surely announce every departure and arrival.

Breakfast Diplomacy

IN 1991, a weeklong train ride on the Trans-Siberian Railway required careful meal planning on the part of the passengers. The dining car shifted cuisine with each country, so supplementing meal options was advised. These were the waning days of the Soviet Union, and the longest stretch of time on the train was with a Russian dining car. Supplies had been known to grow scarce, uninspiring at best.

My mother and I traveled west from Beijing to Moscow. At the time, Beijing had a grocery store in the embassy district, where we selected items with prized travel characteristics: durability, portability, and variety. Bags of oranges and packets of roasted pumpkin seeds, as well as all the imported chocolate we could track down. Sleeves of crackers were added to our basket, as were several clutches of bananas—all smaller and sweeter than those we were accustomed to in the States. Mom, ever prepared, had brought string grocery bags, so we arrived at the Beijing train station laden as if we planned to turn our compartment into a corner store.

Once aboard the train, my romantic fantasy of bejeweled passengers was dashed. This was a train filled with wheelers and dealers freighting knock-off clothing and cheap electronics between the two capital cities and parceling out their wares at various outposts along the route. Our compartment, however, felt like a penthouse, given its comfortable sleeping bunks, washroom, and table for two by the window. No red velvet cushions or tinkling crystal, but no matter. Compared to my recent rides, this was the high life.

I spent much of the trip with my Russian-English dictionary clamped in one hand, boxing up and putting in storage all the Chinese vocabulary I had spent the last semester cramming into my brain. Sentences that had been a cinch a year earlier were linguistic crossed wires. I now spoke Russian like a Neanderthal might.

Food good.
Me Anita.

My resurrected Russian was not the only thing that felt new. While I had gotten us on the train in one piece, the process had been beset by weather delays and anxieties about travel visas, and I was still reeling from the experience. For the first time in my life I had stepped into the role of parent: managing preparations in Beijing, taking care of all our on-the-ground details, and explaining the culture I now understood to my mother. She acclimated to the role reversal far better than I did. Her equanimity during pre-travel hiccups contrasted with my shorter temper. After spending the last six months at the greatest distance we had ever been apart, Mom and I now faced each other across a table the size of a checkerboard with an entire week ahead of us. I spent the first day recovering my wits, likely under my headphones, a behavior that now seems uncharitable at best. Over the next six days on the train, Mom caught me up on the news from home, filling in the spaces that our letters back and forth did not cover. I told her stories about my new friends and China highlights as I began to introduce her to the person I was becoming.

When our train heaved and hissed into Moscow early in the morning a week later, our grocery bags were nearly empty and we were ready to stretch our legs beyond the corridors of a train. Our host, Igor, met us on a platform that thrummed with people even at the early hour. Sky peeked through the vaulted brickwork and the intercom solemnly announced departures. The train station was just a few miles from the city center, and we were soon driving toward Igor's home in one of the many nondescript concrete apartment blocks so representative of the vision many in the West had of Soviet utilitarian architecture. We made our way through the drab environs to the apartment. No landscaping surrounded the collection of concrete high rises. The unlit stairwell led to landings with intimidating wrought-iron outer doors on each apartment that gave the impression of a prison.

Yet when Igor swung open the inner door to his home, the brightly lit and colorful interior was as inviting as the exterior was bleak. Tables were pushed together for breakfast, and his wife and friends greeted us as if it were our long-anticipated homecoming.

We feasted on hard-boiled eggs, cucumbers, and slices of tomato half the size of tomatoes I grew up eating and twice as tasty. Dark brown bread was accompanied by butter and pickled onions. Strong coffee was on hand, and even stronger vodka.

Igor and his wife, Luba, were patient with my Russian and hospitable. I cobbled sentences together between bites of breakfast, vocabulary returning with the gentle encouragement of those around me. There was friendly inquisitiveness about my time in China, our lives in the United States, and our desire that the arms race between the Soviet Union and the United States would be halted. In this land still governed by a political philosophy that placed the collective above the individual, the communal spaces were unremarkable and the individual homes had a vibrancy that rejected conformity.

None of us knew that the Soviet Union would fracture five months later, but when I look back on our short time in the country, I realize signs were evident. The ruble was in free fall. Mom and I dined at a restaurant in Moscow where the bill came to under one US dollar for two bowls of soup, thin Russian pancakes called *bliny*, and multiple meat entrées. The following week in Riga, abandoned barricades from recent Latvian independence protests obstructed the middle of major thoroughfares. The pressure for reform was brewing.

The locked horns of the Soviet Union and the United States had been a political reality my entire life—and most of my mother's, for that matter. On that first morning in Moscow, to toast our new acquaintance and a hope for these individual diplomatic efforts, Igor poured a round of vodka. I gamely tossed back my shot. Having never seen my mother take a drink, I made eye contact with her and she nodded nearly imperceptibly with gratitude. The burn of her serving of vodka traveled my mouth to my stomach like a lit fuse. This act told my mother that the gratitude was all mine.

I spent the first seven weeks of 2013 living a stone's throw from the Pantheon. I was in Rome to co-teach a course on culture and communication.

My home base was a restored apartment off Rome's Palazzo Pio, a multi-story building with sections dating back to the thirteenth century. My apartment had soaring ceilings, tiled floors, and tall windows with slatted shutters that could hook shut from the inside. Cloud formations and the Mediterranean light turned my windows into framed Maxfield Parrish paintings.

Rome elevates the commonplace to art.

Nearby church bells chimed the hours, marking the movement of morning to night. While I knew visitors arrived in Rome and became rapturous about the pace, the food, and the irresistible concealed pockets of the city, I was still impressed by how quickly Rome bewitched me. Each time I threw open the shutters and took in the rooftop view of the city, I half expected animated bluebirds to perch on my fingers as if I starred in my very own Disney movie.

Feeding the Neighborhood

WHEN IN ROME, I walked and walked. I could not get enough of the cobblestone streets fanning out for miles like mosaic fractals. It was January, so in some neighborhoods the narrow streets were still strung overhead with white lights left hanging from Christmas, creating an illuminated cat's cradle that helped shepherd me home. The streets led me to markets, dance classes, and every gelateria I could find. These destinations tested my beginner language skills as well as my beginner understanding of Italian culture. Supermarkets looked similar to those in the United States, but crucial differences—like the protocol of weighing and marking your produce before getting rung up at the cashier—exposed me as an interloper. The first time I visited a local dance studio it took twenty minutes to find the right room, and the sting of incomprehension left me sheepish as I asked the front desk to repeat directions to me once again, *per favore*. The humiliation in those moments was total. *Gelaterie*, on the other hand, posed no problem. If words failed me, I could point.

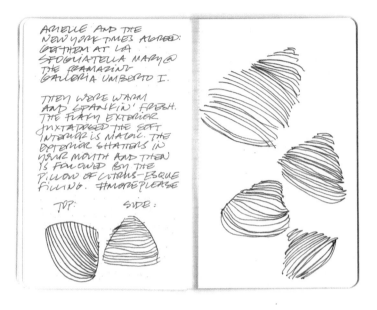

ARIELLE AND THE
NEW YORK TIMES AGREED:
GET THEM AT LA
SFOGLIATELLA MARY @
THE RAMAZINT
GALLERIA UMBERTO I.

THEY WERE WARM
AND SPANKIN' FRESH.
THE FLAKY EXTERIOR
JUXTAPOSED THE SOFT
INTERIOR IS MAGIC. THE
EXTERIOR SHATTERS IN
YOUR MOUTH AND THEN
IS FOLLOWED BY THE
PILLOW OF CITRUS-ESQUE
FILLING. #MOREPLEASE

TOP: SIDE:

UMBRELLA
TREES
OF
ROME.

22 GENNAIO, 2013

Side streets were paths to hidden troves: a small piazza, a stringed-instrument repair shop, or a courtyard where oranges hung heavily from potted trees. The Italians even made upholstery shops glamorous with elegant window dressing. Once I came upon a woman drying homemade *orecchiette*, "little ears" pasta that forms small indentations for holding sauce. She sent me off with a bag. I returned to Seattle with holes worn into the heels of my socks and the habit of a morning cappuccino.

My walks often involved meals. Sometimes they were as quick as a slab of mushroom pizza eaten while standing at the marble counter of a corner pizzeria. There were cozy family restaurants in my neighborhood that started you off with flutes of prosecco, no need to ask—these were the meals that wound sedately over multiple courses and conversations. I bit into *carciofi fritti*, artichokes smashed and then deep-fried, and spun my fork and spoon into a plate of *fettuccine al limone*, a yellow nest of unadorned pasta so divine that I nearly tossed my napkin to the table and burst into the kitchen, demanding to meet the magician behind my swoon. And pasta was just a starter—a pause between the *antipasti* and *secondi* courses. Walking was the best way to see Rome and also how I built an appetite worthy of these meals.

Meals in Italy beguiled well beyond Rome. For over a decade, my friend Arielle, an Italianist, spouted streams of praise for Naples. Arielle and I met in high school, when she was her own version of a René Magritte painting, long-stemmed black umbrella and all. She was often the first to class and the smartest in the room. After years spent in Italy, she traded her surrealist uniform for couture. Arielle now brings a Milanese catwalk look to a short trip to her corner store in her high heels, flowing linen, and necklaces. She hooked me with stories of this jewel of a city on the Tyrrhenian Sea, easing my worries about the political dysfunction and mafia stereotypes. Naples sounded much like the Philadelphia of my childhood, its seductions tainted by a somewhat ill-deserved reputation. I was excited for the chance to see a bit of grit in this land where such emphasis was placed on a cultivated aesthetic.

Taking Arielle's passion for Naples to heart, my colleague Nancy and I took a scouting trip to prepare for when we would take our students. We spent a night crisscrossing the city as we ate our way through *la bella Napoli*.

We tested *sfogliatelle*, a seashell-shaped pastry that crumbles in your mouth. We sampled *un caffè* pulled by gearshift-like levers from an imposing espresso machine at Caffè Mexico with a statue of Dante looking sternly down upon us, arm outstretched, from the piazza that bears his name. We sipped *falanghina*, a white wine with a name traced back to the Latin word *falangae*, the vineyard stakes used to buttress the grapes. We indulged in a *pizza margherita* hot from the oven, the basil and tomatoes submerged in bubbling mozzarella from the hallowed Pizzaria Gina Sobrillo.

The meal that topped all others was at Da Enzo's, Arielle's go-to eatery for pasta in Naples. Even though she had eaten there week in and week out during her first residence in the city in the early nineties, she could only provide a few details: the name of the neighborhood, the restaurant's location relative to an *ospedale* (say it out loud) and a *mercatino*, and that you entered via, of all things, a storage room. Since Italians share their streets with hoards of tourists

IN BARI, THERE ARE SOME TRADITIONAL DISHES THAT YOU DO NOT WANT TO MISS. ONE OF THEM IS

ORECHIETTA CON RAPE *

THESE PASTA PIECES ARE CALLED "LITTLE EARS" AND THE RAPE/RAPA ARE THE ENDS OF TURNIP GREENS:

*PRONOUNCED RAH-PAY

CHOP CHOP CHOP!

THE ORECHIETTA ARE LIKE LITTLE CUPS THAT HUG THE SAUCE MADE FROM THE PUREED GREENS:

JUST ABOUT THIS SIZE!

CAFE DA ENZO —
14 GENNAIO, 2013

THE LIGHT FROM DA ENZO WAS IMMEDIATELY WELCOMING. I LOOKED INSIDE: CHECKED BLUE TABLECLOTHS/ I MEAN♥ CHECKED BLUE. THE TABLES ARE CHEEK TO JOWL — YOU FEEL AS IF YOU SHOULD INTRODUCE YOURSELF TO YOUR NEIGHBORS.

I HAD ALREADY SCOPED OUT THE MENU AND KNEW THAT I WAS GOING TO ORDER THE CARBONARA. I WAS USED TO THE DISH BEING PRESENTED WITH SPAGHETTI AND SMALL CHUNKS OF BACON.

OMG.

NOT THIS CARBONARA!

HUGE PASTA PIECES AND HUGE CHUNKS OF BACON SO SALT-CURED AND PERFECTLY PAN-FRIED I WANTED TO WEEP.

I WANTED TO SAVOR EVERY BITE!

most of the year, you cannot blame them for wanting to keep some things out of sight. We had no street name, no phone number, and no question that we were going to find this place.

What we found is that Da Enzo's feeds its neighborhood. Tables were set with blue and white paper tablecloths. The menu, recited in person once we were seated, consisted of four pasta dishes, two vegetable side dishes, water, and house wine. A basket of fresh bread was also provided. The kitchen was the size of a closet. A freshly caught octopus sat plopped on the counter as if taking a nap in preparation for its starring role in dinner. As the lunch hour approached, regulars announced their arrival by calling out greetings to the kitchen. As in a neighborhood diner, patrons ranged from retirees to working professionals. Many shouted their orders before even taking their seat.

At times, travel asks us to play the imposter—we shape-shift with varying degrees of success, waiting for the inevitable exposure. The chance of me fading into the background is higher in southern Italy than, say, northern Pakistan, where no scarf could swaddle my features enough to avoid detection. Da Enzo's gave me the illusion of local access. We were cordially treated like everyone else, with efficient service and no rush to finish.

My *spaghetti alle vongole* was the best I have ever tasted. Each dainty clam was the size of a locket, split open like a pair of hands clapping for me as I twirled fresh pasta onto my fork. Napoli peppers gave the dish some heat, and the wonderfully chewy bread sopped up the butter garlic sauce.

Sadly, all good meals must end. But meals can be logged for posterity in many ways. A few years ago I started sketchnoting them as a way to relive and recall the memory. This suited my interest in how observation serves memory, and all I needed was a pen and paper. Documenting my meals makes me appreciate them in a new way and lets me share them with others not at my table.

I rarely left my Rome home without pen and paper, never knowing where my next meal might appear. Chefs put their creativity on the plate, and I translated it to the page. My sketchnotes were an alchemy of the pen, transforming what I consumed into what I would long remember. A fork feeds my appetite; a pen feeds my memory.

Meals were not the only memories of Italy I wanted to safeguard. I felt a harmony with city living, a compatibility with my smaller apartment footprint combined with the locomotion my willing feet provided me. Within a year of leaving Rome, I had sold my car and downsized from a house to a condo in Seattle. My world expanded as I sought small.

Pacific Northwest light forms its own superior painting against the clouds beyond my Seattle windows. Artistry is everywhere when we look closely.

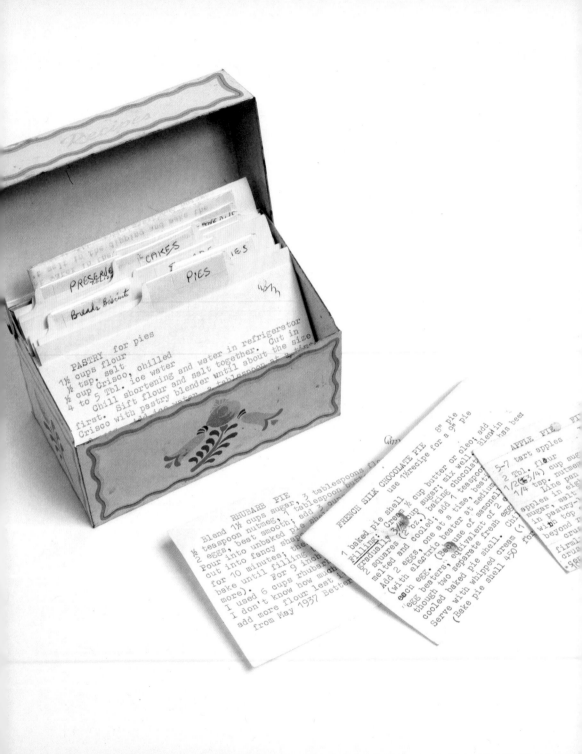

PRESERV... CAKES PIES Breads Biscuit

PASTRY for pies
1½ cups flour
½ tsp. salt
¼ cup Crisco, chilled
4 to 5 Tbl. ice water
  Chill shortening and water in refrigerator
first. Sift flour and salt together. Cut in
Crisco with pastry blender until about the size...

RHUBARB PIE
  Blend 1½ cups sugar, 3 tablespoons flour,
¼ teaspoon nutmeg, 1 tablespoon ...
2 eggs, beat smooth; add 3 cups ...
Pour into unbaked pie shell ...
cut into fancy shap...
for 10 minutes; the...
bake until filling...
more).   For 9 inch...
  I used 6 cups rhubar...
I don't know how much ...
add more flour lest i...
     from May 1937 Better...

FRENCH SILK CHOCOLATE PIE   9" pie
1 baked pie shell   use ½ recipe for a 9" pie
Filling: Cream ½ cup butter or oleo; add
gradually ¾ cup sugar; mix well. Blend in
2 squares (2 oz.) baking chocolate,
melted and cooled; add 1 teaspoon ...
  Add 2 eggs, one at a time, beat...
(with electric beater at medium ...
each egg. (Because of samonell...
'egg beaters, equivalent of 2 eg...
though two separate fresh egg...
cooled baked pie shell. Chill ...
Serve with whipped cream (1 ...
  (Bake pie shell 450 fo...

APPLE PIE   FI...
5-7 tart apples
2 Tbl. flour
½ (1/3/4) cup suga...
¼ tsp. nutmeg...
     Line pan...
apples in eig...
sugar, salt...
in pastry...
with top...
beyond r...
       crus...
firmly...
crus...
'99...

Pie

Pie making is my inheritance. My maternal grandmother passed her prowess along to my mother, and they both bequeathed their pie powers to me. I keep a metal box of typed recipes my grandmother gave me in the baking drawer of one of my kitchen cabinets. The pie section includes a number that are smeared with butter and cinnamon. A stained recipe card signals a well-loved recipe.

Pies are cousins to empanadas, panzerotti, and galettes, yet distinguish themselves by their unmatched range of flavors. Pies suit any meal—warm pie for dessert means cold pie for breakfast, if there is any left. Their flexibility is part of their popularity. Recently, as yet another new pie store opened in my Seattle neighborhood, I mused that pies have dethroned cupcakes as the hot new baked good. Regardless, in my family, pie has always been in style.

The Problem with Crisco

THE FIRST PROBLEM with Crisco is that it makes such a fantastic piecrust. My mother and grandmother made the pies I loved best growing up—most notably apple—with Crisco crusts that dissolved with traces of salty splendor on my tongue. My mom even kept a cup of the white stuff chilled in the fridge so a piecrust would always be at the ready. Crisco was a convenience. In the 1970s, it was viewed as a healthier alternative to lard. Which brings me to its second problem. Crisco is not healthy at all. Hydrogenated oils have gone from the darlings of the food world to the villains.

I cannot claim this crust epiphany as my own. My education arrived thanks to my friend Jess, who often acts as my food conscience. Jess is a walking RSS feed, curating nuggets of information I should not miss. Her intelligence around my preferences is time-tested and guarantees that I listen. I scrub my fruit and vegetables with a special cleansing wash because of Jess. I skip chicken unless I know who raised the bird because of Jess. And, because of Jess, I vowed to learn how to make a piecrust out of butter. Even with my hereditary pie-making mojo, I was utterly intimidated by his prospect.

Butter is a fickle thing. When I switched from Crisco I was already schooled in pie assemblage and knew that the fat must be chilled for a successful crust. During my first attempts I worked the butter too hard without letting the dough rest before I wielded my rolling pin. Instead of shattering into a crumble of buttery goodness, these crusts fought the fork when you ate them.

But I was not deterred. I persisted, and each butter crust was better than the last. My friends Ken and Kristy helped hone my craft by suggesting we hold a quarterly homemade Pie Day. This idea was in keeping with their enjoyment of all things gastronomic: they are the kind of people who organize wild mushroom hunts, host themed supper clubs, and know all the best places to pick blackberries in August. When Ken married, his wife Gina made us a baking quartet. All kinds of pies made appearances at Pie Day. Apple crumble or pumpkin bacon in autumn. Blackberry or ginger peach pie in summer. Kristy once brought a pecan pie that was so sweet even just the smallest slice produced a sugar rush. My grandmother's chocolate silk pie was trumpeted for its decadence. Ken introduced us to pasties, a Michigan meat and potato hand pie that arrived in the Upper Peninsula with waves of English immigrants. I made my first chicken pot pie for a Pie Day. We never coordinated beforehand, preferring to marvel at the results born of kismet.

Another part of Pie Day was the affability. Pie, in general, invites company. A single pie can easily feed eight or even stretch to sixteen slices. I have also seen two people do serious damage to a single pie. My pies have shown up in my classrooms to herald the end of a term, flown cross-country, and been delivered by bicycle in a tiffin. Wherever and however, pie should be shared.

A butter crust now feels as straightforward as cracking an egg in a pan. Continuing the generational transfer of pie knowledge, I walked my goddaughter through the steps, and she baked an apple pie to perfection. A natural. The crust of my childhood was nowhere to be seen, but my grandmother and mother's influence was everywhere.

My work with the University of Washington Department of Global Health took me to Sudan a half dozen times between 2008 and 2012. I was part of a team that delivered trainings for health professionals on the themes of leadership, management, and policy. My contributions revolved around visual communication, digital storytelling, and communication styles.

Sudan rubs geographic shoulders with the Middle East, is the site of the confluence of the White and Blue Niles, and shares a border with seven countries. It is home to a diverse indigenous population and has housed travelers from across the region for millennia. Sudan's capital, Khartoum, is the nexus of this intermingling.

A Sudanese Minute

KHARTOUM is a sleepy capital city. Its side streets are lined with willow trees, and five times a day calls to prayer pierce the otherwise quiet air. Few tall buildings compete with the sky, and much of the city is comprised of residential compounds no more than three stories tall.

The city feels like a sigh of repose.

The natural world is more visible amidst all that is man-made. Incoming dust storms clearly advance toward the city from miles away, and proximity to the desert defines this urban oasis. Sand the color of a new penny and as fine as flour sneaks into every crevice and collects like dust on tabletops, patios, and car dashboards. Brooms are always in use in Khartoum. The temperature can shift severely, dipping at night and rising to oven-like blasts throughout the day. Whenever the warm desert air greeted me as I stepped off a plane in Khartoum, flip-flops came out and socks went into my suitcase for the rest of my stay.

We joked during our trainings about the difference between a Sudanese minute and an American minute. Place your thumb and finger an inch apart and you have the latter. Now throw your arms as wide as your wingspan allows, and welcome to Sudan.

While I kept my eyes on the time during meetings and trainings, over meals it was another story altogether. Time slowed when food was on the table. No one knew this better than Wisal, a Sudanese graduate of the University of Washington with a radiance that rivaled the sun. I counted on her to be my restaurant guide.

Evening excursions took place when work was done for the day and the heat had abated, replaced by cool desert night. We used fingers to pull apart *samak mashwi*, grilled freshwater fish, served with key limes and a piquant dipping sauce. A hibiscus iced tea, *karkaday*, slaked parched mouths. Then there were meals of spiced grilled lamb with fresh wheels of bread and peppery arugula, accompanied by bowls of *foul sudani*, a hearty fava bean stew—think Sudanese chili. Always up for dessert, we would relocate to a café smack in the middle of a busy Khartoum roundabout, where you had a dizzying selection of gelato, single-serving cakes, fruit tarts, and coffee. The wide outdoor couches were made for lounging, and time unspooled as we were lulled by the shallow croons of circling three-wheeled jitneys. On weekends we returned to the café's couches, protected from the sun by yawning umbrellas and a system of ingenious mist-makers that kept customers cool, as though we were produce needing protection from wilting in the heat.

My joy in Sudanese dining extended far beyond what was on my plate. It also included the simplicity of the ingredients, the Sudanese emphasis on hospitality, and their unhurried manner. I was treated to barbecue on the outskirts of the city, where diced meat was grilled right in front of you and presented with an onion, tomato, and cucumber salad to keep it company, along with a small bowl of sea salt, puffed pillows of bread, and green chili dipping sauce. I ate these meals seated on iron bedframes webbed with twine so that after overeating I had the option to recline and take a nap. I have been tempted by plates of *kisrah*, a sorghum flour pancake widely available from street vendors, and paired it with a shot-glass amount of coffee spiced with ginger, cardamom, and cinnamon. I often passed on sugar for my coffee, which drew bemused reactions from my Sudanese colleagues. I enjoyed that many meals were served communally on aluminum trays, and how I had to lean in close to eat. Sudanese colleagues were eager to introduce me to their tastes of home, and the meals lasted for hours.

Sudan fed my curiosity, and its relationship with time prompted reflection. What was I missing? Was I moving too fast? What might surface if I did not rush to talk over all the quiet? I left Sudan full every time.

中华人民共和国

外国人旅行证

The People's Republic of China

Aliens' Travel Permit

43B 字第 930495 号

No.

After college I received a travel fellowship that funded a sixteen-month photography and ethnography project in China. Happily, I now had an answer to the dreaded question, "What are you going to do after you graduate?" even though I had not thought much beyond buying a thirty-five millimeter camera, sturdy backpack, and plane ticket.

My new residence in China began in Kunming, the provincial capital of Yunnan Province in the southwest part of the country. Known as the Spring City for its enviable weather, Kunming sits more than a mile above sea level, with the edge of the Himalayas to the north and the jungles of the Golden Triangle of Burma, Laos, and Thailand to the south.

Favorable climates produce a plentitude of fresh food. Kunming introduced me to the benefits of a year-round growing season, as well as the restaurant practice of having customers order off the kitchen shelves after scanning what was bought from the market that day. Choices often included buckets of eels, baskets of foraged mushrooms, various plates of greens, meats, and basins piled with freshly washed *báiyún dòu*, the marvelously named "white cloud" beans. Surveying inventory in a restaurant kitchen instead of ordering off a menu inspired new combinations of ingredients—a bricolage approach to dining.

Meals were portals into my newest Chinese community, which took shape differently in this city than it had during my earlier sojourns in Beijing and Nanjing. A northern formality was replaced with a refreshing southern ease—helped by my improving language skills. Connecting over food and drink helped foster a rapport I had not often experienced with Chinese peers. The state, watchful after the events in Tiananmen Square, had hovered over my first two stays in China and made contact with Chinese peers more fraught. I welcomed this change.

Meet Me at the Bamboo Table

COFFEE SHOPS are now common in Kunming, but such things were virtually unheard of when I lived there in 1992. It was hard to find a coffee shop anywhere in China, though Folgers instant coffee was widely available. The single-serving packets included freeze-dried milk and sugar, producing a cup of coffee that was the equivalent of a liquid candy bar. While it satisfied my sweet tooth, I did not consider the drink real coffee.

Nanlaisheng Coffee and Bread Shop was the exception to Kunming's café vacuum. It was located on a tree-lined street in an older section of the city, and its neighboring shops hawked everything from intricate bamboo birdcages to rag mops. The coffee shop was written up in a favored travel guide, but it was the locals who tipped me off. For the first time while living in China, I had made close Chinese friends.

Yang Haiyu and Zhai Wen were college students at Yunnan University, where I lived in a guesthouse reserved for foreigners. (At the time it was nearly impossible to rent a private apartment, as employers still by and large owned and assigned residences. These rules would change within a year or two.) Yang Haiyu spoke in torrents of fluent English with a facility for slang that slayed me. When he found something funny, his face cracked in half like a Muppet, eyes creased with joy in explosive laughter. His best friend, Zhai Wen, had a steady delivery that complemented Yang Haiyu's verbal rapids. We traded music on cassette tapes, played cards in my apartment, and watched bootleg movies from aspiring Chinese filmmakers. Loosely translated, Yang Haiyu's given name means "ocean and universe," and Zhai Wen's translates to "a question." These meanings matched our shared circumstances and stages in life: questioning the ocean and universe of possibilities before us.

China was changing fast, and so were we. I was in between college and career, unsure of what I wanted to do when I grew up. Yang Haiyu and Zhai Wen were members of the first class of college seniors in China since the 1960s who were not automatically assigned a job by the state upon graduation. The implications of this policy adjustment cannot be overstated. Reforms in the mid-1990s presented people with choices that had been unavailable for decades, and such freedom was both eagerly anticipated and nerve-racking. Zhai Wen and Yang Haiyu were facing the same unknowns as I was—almost unimaginable to those just five years older.

Our first visit to Nanlaisheng was eye-opening. Far from campus, this was not a coffee shop frequented by undergraduates. Most customers were Chinese

men over the age of seventy. The shop's white-tiled walls resembled a subway platform—a design choice that was all the rage in China at the time. Chairs scuffed across the tile floor as customers came and went. The offerings were limited: bracing drip coffee and French-style demi-baguettes as hard as door-knobs. You placed your order at the front of the shop and took your triplicate coupon the size of a raffle ticket to the back to be filled. Discarded tickets littered the floor. Coffee was served in gray ceramic mugs with no handles. Many were worn and chipped, though no one cared. It was fresh coffee in the land of tea.

The coffee was local. French colonizers established coffee plantations in northern Vietnam and southern Yunnan, just across the Vietnamese border. The climate was suited for the bean, and soon the French laid a narrow-gauge railroad between Yunnan and Hanoi in large part to move beans to city roasters. While coffee took hold firmly in Vietnam, tea still ruled supreme in China. But in Kunming's Nanlaisheng, coffee had staged a successful coup.

While trips to Nanlaisheng were rare, my forays with Yang Haiyu and Zhai Wen to quiet rumbling stomachs happened often. They introduced me to Kunming's outdoor night markets, where vendors strung lights and packed small tables into congenial clusters for night owls with an appetite. We chomped fried pig ears, nibbled skewers of *chòu dòufu* ("stinky tofu") dusted with chili powder, and slurped *mǐxiàn*, rice noodles in broth so spicy it made me gasp and paw for my water glass in a desperate attempt to wash the fire down my throat. Wheat noodles hold court in northern China and rice noodles command the south.

Feasts were not limited to after hours. Lunch might find us with fresh pineapple pops scored and sliced by vendors wielding cleavers as delicately as scalpels. These tastes of the tropics were also used as a vessel for steaming purple rice and paired with grilled fish wrapped in banana leaves. Tiny restaurants near campus that catered to a student budget were perennial favorites. We would split a liter of Pepsi and wolf down wok-fried and peppered slices of *rŭbĭng*, a hard goat cheese; spicy lotus root sliced thin to reveal lace-like patterns; pickled mustard root with red beans; and *tŭdòusī*, shaved threads of potatoes pan-fried with vinegar and peppers. The volley of conversation kept pace with the arrival of each dish, a meal that felt like the building block of a manifesto on how life should be. The three of us championed each other's paths to glory.

When I left Kunming to return to the United States, Yang Haiyu gave me a gift: a miniature bamboo table with matching chairs. The set was the perfect size for a family of mice or, in my case, a woman traveling light. He included a note: "No matter where you are, we will always be able to meet around this table, share a meal, and talk." From that time forward, "meet me at the bamboo table" was our valediction. The table was a motivator and a placeholder until our next anticipated meal in person, which at the time seemed about as certain as us dining together on the moon.

Years later, Yang Haiyu wrote to say that Nanlaisheng's picturesque street had been widened, sacrificing the stately trees and the shops. By then, this was common practice across China as neighborhoods were leveled to accommodate the country's growing obsession with automobiles. Roads represented

mobility and progress, and China was awash with ambition. But no matter how many new roads were built, the pace of construction could not keep up with the pace of consumption, and city streets today are choked with traffic.

Both Yang Haiyu and Zhai Wen launched their entrepreneurial careers within the nascent nonprofit sector, which provided both a fair degree of independence and international travel. My own career began when I swapped Philadelphia for Seattle, trading a city steeped in my country's past for one hell-bent on writing its future.

That future involved technology, and the technology changed the way my friends and I communicated. Letters became e-mails, then videoconferences, and now social media. Our sign-off, though, remained the same no matter the method: "meet me at the bamboo table." Part marker of a stage in our lives that was rich in possibility and part wishful thinking, the words knit meals and memory together.

WE ALL REUNITED when I returned to Kunming in 2014. Nanlaisheng reopened not far from its first location, so Zhai Wen and I set off to investigate. What we found was dissimilar from the past in every way: a coffee house ("shop" does not do justice to the décor) that you entered via an elevator as if you were a member of an exclusive club. The elevator opened onto a room filled with mahogany booths and an extended rooftop deck with shaded tables. The drinks were as varied as the old café's were limited. Gone were the rough, battered coffee mugs. Most customers were under thirty and oozed urbanity.

This upscale coffee experience is not exclusive to China. When one seeks a cup of coffee today, it is easy to be overwhelmed by the selection. The new Nan-laisheng represents something far larger than consumerism. Yang Haiyu and Zhai Wen build lives today—as do I—that are a testament to the advantages of self-determination, combined with economic development and access. Plans hatched over meals in our twenties continue to fuel us as we enter middle age. My return to Kunming included as many meals as we could fit in, starting with a huge bowl of *mǐxiàn*.

Do I miss the China of my twenties? Certainly, I miss parts keenly—though I know the passage of time applies a nostalgic filter, even at the expense of reality. Intimate residential alleys, mobile food carts, and a chorus of bike bells all form a Chinese landscape, foodscape, and soundscape that are fast disappearing, if not gone already. But amenities come with new home construction, some street food is now on restaurant menus, and cars cover more ground. Furthermore, the meals Yang Haiyu, Zhai Wen, and I share today are as suffused with flavor and conversation as they were when we first met. Progress applies to each of us as well, and our better selves appear with each new year and meal.

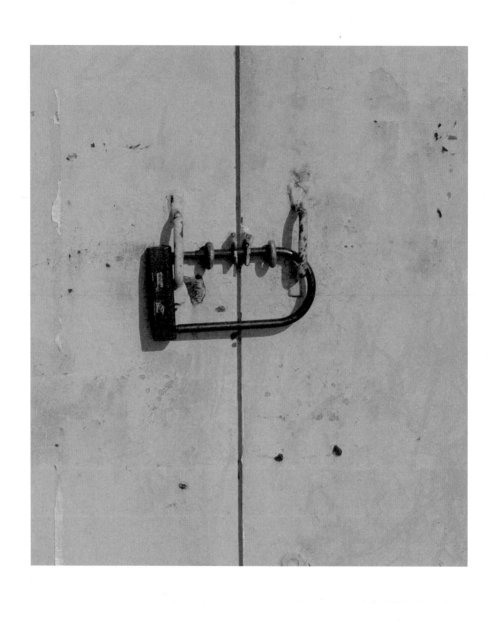

My pre-flight ritual when I leave Seattle rarely varies: once I clear security, I order a tall extra-dark hot chocolate at Dilettante Chocolates in the main food court. The time of day and season do not matter. I crave hot chocolate before takeoff. I return again and again for the reassurance of ritual and also because their hot chocolate tastes intense, yet not too sweet. The chocolate flavor does not sing backup for the sugar. Hot chocolate is my travel rite to slow my brain down in preparation for my body's imminent velocity.

In the spring of 2003, velocity was my middle name. An around-the-world ticket had kept me on the move since December 2002. I started in the southern hemisphere and made my way north. I had long wanted to see Scandinavia. My paternal great-grandmother was a Swedish-speaking Finn, and though she lived much of her adult life oceans away from Finland, I still felt a genealogical pull to see the region. And I had never met a Swedish pancake I did not love.

Chocolate Cup

I LANDED IN SWEDEN at a postage stamp of an airport an hour and a half from Stockholm after a night of very little sleep. Cheap air travel within Europe necessitates a sacrifice: secondary airports are often miles from civilization, so an early morning departure means setting an alarm for the dead of night. Sweden graciously provided tour buses to meet each plane, so I dozed as I rode into the city where my friend Sharon, a transplant from Indonesia living in Stockholm (by way of Seattle), awaited me. Though it was spring in Scandinavia, it snowed when I arrived. The charter bus and snowflakes seemed Sweden's way of offering me a welcome wrapped in a challenge.

The snow made a hasty exit by afternoon and left me a city that soaked up the sun. Stockholm is an infinitely walkable town. Its narrow alleys and wide plazas were draped with humans when the sun shone—the Swedes popped out like heat-seeking lizards. This was understandable given the winter months they spent manufacturing light to shoo away nineteen hours of darkness a day.

Nary a Swedish meatball was seen in my first dinners in Stockholm. The first two meals were what you might expect in many bustling metropolitan areas: take-out sushi and Thai dining by tiki torch light. A few nights later we ate around an Ethiopian *mesob*, a woven basket that served as a table. A large round tray was placed on top of the basket, blanketed completely with *injera*, an Ethiopian sourdough flatbread that doubled as a plate for the various main courses spooned atop it. We tore swatches of this oversized crêpe with our fingers, as is customary, to scoop up mouthfuls of *doro wat,* a spicy chicken stew often served with hard-boiled eggs; *shiro,* a powdered garbanzo bean stew; and toothsome *tibs,* or sautéed meat.

The presence of East African food in Stockholm, seven thousand miles from Addis Ababa, was not simply the result of an expanding Swedish appetite. It was due to an expanding population of immigrants. Some of the first were from neighboring Nordic countries after World War II as Sweden industrialized. This wave grew to include job seekers from the European Union and asylum seekers from South America and the Middle East. Today, numbers are swelling with more recent arrivals from Central Europe, East Africa, and the Middle East. The stereotype of Swedes as blond-haired and blue-eyed Vikings needs updating.

Sweden has a long history of exploration and settlement in new lands. Swedish-speaking Finnish nationals date back to the twelfth century and the First Swedish Crusade. My paternal great-grandmother, Verna Hammarén Crofts, was one of them. Born in 1863, Verna was raised in Helsinki. Faith and courage

led her to leave her family in 1893 and travel to China, where she met my Ohio-born great-grandfather. Both missionaries, the two wed in 1899 and over the next seven years had four children, the eldest being my grandfather. In 1904, the family moved to the isolated interior of China, a landscape straight from a Tang dynasty scroll: wooded mountains rose from rivers, and ceramic-tiled pagodas peeped through the foliage. It took months by boat to reach the coast from their secluded home in Guizhou Province, so it was a trip not taken often. In 1909, after one such journey to accompany her three eldest children to boarding school on the coast, Verna contracted dysentery and died, leaving five heartbroken family members, four under the age of ten. She had returned to Finland from China only once, on furlough.

Swedish-speaking Finns communicate in a dialect that allows them to order food effortlessly in Stockholm. I thought of my great-grandmother the night that Sharon and I partook of a smorgasbord deserving of the name: four kinds of silvery herring, meatballs smothered in gravy, side dishes of pickled cucumbers and tart lingonberry compote, and *knäckebröd*, a cracker-like bread the size and stiffness of a Frisbee. Had I been able to conjure my great-grandmother as translator, I would have, not just for the culinary doors she could open, but also to ask for details about her too-brief life. I wanted to hear about her days in China and what she longed for back in Finland. We could banter in Chinese, which she spoke fluently. (She wrote in a letter to her family in Finland that "the Chinese language is a hard knot for me," a sentiment I understood all too well.) Both of us lived in China in our twenties, and while my time there was a launchpad, she did not live to see the age of fifty.

These daydreams kept me company as I walked Stockholm's sidewalks, foraging for my next meal. Sharon teased that all paths led me to Chokladkoppen, a low-ceilinged café on the ground floor of a golden-colored building facing Stortorget Square in Gamla Stan, the center of Stockholm since the Middle Ages. The first time I visited Chokladkoppen I ordered hot chocolate—often my litmus test for a café. It arrived in a ceramic bowl with a chocolate-syrup heart drizzled in the froth. So far, so good. But hot chocolate need not be high-end looking; what is important is that it is high-end tasting. Chokladkoppen ("chocolate cup") lived up to its name. Strong chocolate notes were my reward each time I raised the bowl for a sip.

From Seattle to Stockholm, hot chocolate is found far and wide, showing the reach of the bean that started as an Aztec brew. Quite the traveler in its own right, this equatorial crop rings the globe and ends up in confections of all kinds. It is not just people who relocate, either by choice or by anguished necessity, and thrive in new lands. Crops cross oceans and put down roots as well, adapting to their new environs. As I drank my Swedish hot chocolate, I tasted this history of edible migration, considering my own family history of leaving, love, and loss.

The magic of my first full summer in Maine never left me, and now I wing back east to the state every June. As my plane descends into Portland, my face is plastered against the tiny window with anticipation. The moment the wheels make contact with the runway is euphoric. It takes all my willpower when we taxi to the gate not to spring from my seat, wrench open the exit door, and jump to the tarmac. Home.

My summers in Maine include stays at a family farmhouse. The views are magnificent, even though the July sun bakes the second-floor kitchen by late afternoon. For most of my life, the kitchen had the same sea glass blue paint job with saucepans that hung from nails on the pantry door, their edges leaving rubbed smiles from years of swinging each time the door opened or closed. The hand crank can opener was bolted above a white antique stove. The porcelain farmhouse sink had separate spigots for hot and cold water. Cracked linoleum flooring was underfoot.

Maine slows my tempo as I downshift from my Seattle schedule and rein-troduce myself to misty morning lake swims, the otherworldly call of the whip-poor-will at dusk, and the terpene smell of sticky white pine boughs. Sandy soil grinds underfoot, reminding me that for all the canopied Maine forests, this is a state in large part defined by its relationship to the ocean. I sit hypnotized by the thick sweeps of kelp, alaria, and bladder wrack that undulate under the salt water and welter against the rocky coastline. Sea foam spumes against the shore, creating naturally carbonated surf that is always cold on my toes. My time in Maine is tidal. No matter how far I recede from its shores, I always return.

Food Fight

IT WAS THE SUMMER after my first year of college and I needed a job. I wanted to live in Maine, so camp counselor was an obvious employment choice even though I had no personal summer camp experience. My first and abiding impression of a camp counselor was Bill Murray in the film *Meatballs*, which I had watched repeatedly. Murray's antics were hilarious, and camp activities enthralled me as if I were watching another species entirely. It was slapstick, outrageous, and exaggerated, but it also looked so *fun*. And I knew there were awkward kids like Rudy Gerner out there. I wanted to be their Bill Murray.

I hit the jackpot when Hidden Valley Camp offered me a job. The owners, Peter and Meg, were a winning team: newly married, complementary, and with boundless energy. I liked them both the minute I met them. Peter was flint and Meg was honeycomb. Together they orchestrated the many moving parts of camp. The camp had everything urban professionals desired for their children, from the range of activities—including stained glass art projects, swimming lessons, and creative writing—to the quintessential Maine location, knotty pine cabins with bunk beds and screen doors banging shut, a lake, and a large decommissioned church bell that rang for mealtimes. That bell was music to my ears.

No one missed mealtimes. Lillian, the camp cook, was already a legend by the time I arrived. She oversaw a small staff with brisk jollity. Lillian could produce winners like pancakes and the requisite peanut butter and jelly station, then wave her whisk like a wand to transform fresh fruit and vegetables. Maine boasted a desirable assortment of edibles. Enormous heads of lettuce with scalloped leaves and lustrous cucumbers became salads. Candy sweet Sun Gold tomatoes and teardrop-shaped onions showed up in soups. Lillian came up with myriad ways to present fresh zucchini and bunches of carrots. When a painter's bucket of plums showed up one afternoon outside the kitchen, there was compote by breakfast. Lillian could make just about anything appetizing to the pickiest camper.

And so was that summer. Camp counseling encouraged a blend of goofball tendencies and attentiveness that played well to my strengths. I needed no invitation to act ridiculous if it helped a camper over the homesickness hump. I taught darkroom photography to all ages and spent many a cool and quiet afternoon meditatively rolling the campers' film and developing towers of reels in tall stainless-steel tanks of chemicals. After evenings off spent in search of ice cream, I gingerly stepped my way through the woods to my bunk, scuffing tree roots and scattering pebbles on a path I managed by feel.

Camp had two traditions on the last day of the second session. First, we lined the driveway and danced as the buses trundled the campers back to their families and the land of concrete jungles, highways, and homework. Second, all counselors and staff sat down in the dining hall—now cavernous without a camper to be seen—for a lobster dinner that Lillian prepared to honor another successful summer. Steamed lobsters with melted butter for dipping, boiled corn on the cob, and warm rolls decorated the long tabletops. We sat on benches shoulder to shoulder, enjoying a physical and emotional closeness that came from supporting one another and our campers all summer. The tables were soon littered with lobster shells, wet wads of sea-stinky napkins, and half-empty perspiring pitchers of water. We polished off the meal and lingered in conversation. Unlike every dinner that came before it that summer, this was one where we could remain seated for as long as we wished, with no kids to usher off to cabins, help wash up, and then read aloud to as bedtime neared.

Peter sat in the middle of the longest table, surveying his and Meg's chosen team. Hundreds of campers had bounded through the dining hall and were now all headed home. His taut countenance slacked. He could finally exhale. I saw him look to his left, grip the handle of a water pitcher, and in one stealthy motion dump it over the head of a veteran counselor to his right.

It was instant pandemonium.

Every pitcher was now a weapon, and everything on the table was quickly in play. We were all on our feet, screaming with laughter and hurling the remains of the meal at one another. We chased each other around the room, our clothes dripping and spirits skyrocketing. For two months we maintained order at mealtimes; now, just this once, disorder gloriously reigned. When the squall passed, I was left panting in disbelief that Peter, our meticulous and exacting leader, had set off such a tinderbox. Already a fan, I was now a devotee.

The campers were not the only ones headed back to cities. My car was soon cruising down Interstate 95 as well. The communal meals of the summer were recreated when I moved from a camp dining hall to a college cafeteria. Both rang with the clatter of meals amid ripples of conversation. Both were the sites of small celebrations and the routine. Contentment abounded.

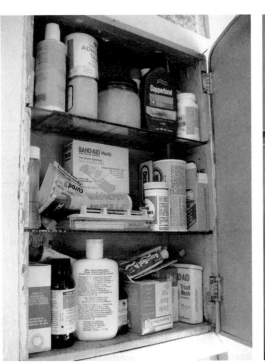 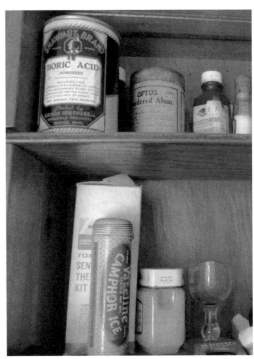

CỘNG HÒA XÃ HỘI CHỦ NGHĨA VIỆT NAM
Socialist Republic of Vietnam

THỊ THỰC số :45082/NQ/93
Visa №

Có giá trị : 01 lần
Valid for

Từ ngày 25/10/1993 đến ngày 25/11/1993 (1)
From to

Họ và tên LEE CHRISTOPHER JUEN-JEN
Full name

Quốc tịch Mỹ
Nationality

Mang hộ chiếu - Giấy Thông hành - Số thuyền viên
holding of Passport - Laisser-Passer - Marine card
số 0.279 56
n°

đi với 1 trẻ em
accompanied by dependant (s)

Họ và tên (s)
Full name (s)

được phép nhập cảnh - nhập xuất cảnh - quá cảnh Việt Nam
is allowed to enter - to enter and exit from - to transit through Vietnam

qua địa điểm NỘI BÀI - TÂN SƠN NHẤT
at frontier point

Cấp tại ngày 26/08/1993
issued at

(1) TOI VIET
25/10/93
25/11/93

LÝ QUỐC TUẦN

ENV 798

CỘNG HÒA XÃ HỘI CHỦ NGHĨA VIỆT NAM
Socialist Republic of Vietnam

THỊ THỰC số :45077/NQ/93
Visa №

Có giá trị : 01 lần
Valid for

Từ ngày 25/10/1993 đến ngày 25/11/1993
From to

Họ và tên CROFTS ANITA VERNA
Full name

Quốc tịch Mỹ
Nationality

Mang hộ chiếu - Giấy Thông hành - Số thuyền viên
holding of Passport - Laisser-Passer - Marine card
số 09 5 440
n°

đi với trẻ em
accompanied by dependant (s)

Họ và tên (s)
Full name (s)

được phép nhập cảnh - nhập xuất cảnh - quá cảnh Việt Nam
is allowed to enter - to enter and exit from - to transit through Vietnam

qua địa điểm NỘI BÀI - TÂN SƠN NHẤT
at frontier point

Cấp tại ngày 26/08/1993
issued at

LÝ QUỐC TUẦN

After calling Kunming, China, home from 1992 to 1993, I embarked with an intrepid itinerary to see the far western reaches of China. I planned to make a big loop and end the calendar year in Vietnam, where the northern overland border with China was open to independent travelers.

I had read Stanley Karnow's *Vietnam: A Nation at War* to better understand the conflict that gripped the United States during the years around my birth in 1970, when grainy images from the war crackled on television screens. I grew up a spectator to the residual injuries of the Vietnam War in the United States—divided opinions, broken bodies and minds of returned soldiers, and the specter of unresolved military engagement. Karnow shifted my aperture on the history of war in Vietnam. He introduced me to the conquering French and their colonial hold on the country in the years before our involvement, and the still earlier history of Chinese invasion and eventual expulsion. This sliver of a country had vanquished invaders many times its own size for centuries. I was curious to see what Vietnam looked like a generation removed from their most recent combat.

New Lightness

IN THE AGE of jet airplanes, I entered Vietnam on foot. I lumbered across the bridge between Hekou, China, and Laocai, Vietnam, looking and moving like a bipedal tortoise, given my substantial backpack and the stifling humidity. I peeled damp dollar bills from my hidden cache to bribe the border patrol, then walked six more kilometers to catch the train that took me to Hanoi.

I arrived in Vietnam with my boyfriend, Chris, whom I had met during a travel fellowship. We spent nearly a year and a half in China, with the most recent five months in wondrous motion out on the western frontier. We traversed mountains in Tibet, cooed at camels in Xinjiang Province, and skidded across landslides in Sichuan. Most days my backpack felt like an extension of my body—I hardly noticed its weight. I ate pounds of *shǒulāmiàn*, hand-pulled noodles fried with tomatoes and cubed meat; demolished flatbread rounds speared from the walls of hot clay ovens; sampled juicy ripe *hāmì guā,* muskmelons; and dialed up my heat tolerance with *huǒguō* ("hot pot"),

a roiling spicy broth for cooking meat and vegetables that Macbeth's witches would have cackled over in appreciation. I was fit and I was on fire. So, too, was my food.

Food is more than answering an appetite's call. The thrill of discovery helps build an appetite, and since Chris and I were first-time visitors to Vietnam, the search was on. Hanoi delivered miracles each time we set out for our next meal: ice cream, cubes of fresh papaya spritzed with limes, and pyramids of *bánh mì*, the fresh baguettes sold on street corners.

Our third night in Hanoi, a friend of a friend invited us to a Buddhist temple where monks and nuns prepared dinner for any interested members of the public. Buddhism first blossomed in northeast Vietnam, with seeds planted by India and China between the first and the third centuries AD. Though firmly established, Buddhists struggled under French colonialism in the first part of the twentieth century, when Catholicism muscled out most of the competition. War with the United States only aggravated the situation, and the arrival of communism in 1975 proved equally challenging. Today, however, there are more relaxed policies around organized religion in Vietnam, and Buddhism is practiced throughout the country.

That evening most of the nuns were on assignment in remote locations, so we found ourselves guests of the head monk, eating from small bowls of vegetarian options and sitting cross-legged on a king-sized raised bed that served as a table. A large bowl of rice and a plate of fresh herbs accompanied soups and cooked vegetables. The meal ended with peeled fruit, strong tea, and a temple tour. The airy chambers were spotless and bright—a far cry from the window-less warrens of the candlelit temples we saw in Tibet.

I fell asleep that night to happy thoughts of my next meal. It turned out I would eat hardly a thing for another week.

I woke in the middle of the night with a spiking fever. Nothing would stay down. Nothing was denied exit. My teeth rattled, my gut heaved, and I dreamed fitfully, waking up periodically to vomit a spectacular shade of bright green. Bacillary dysentery toppled me from the pedestal of healthy invincibility. It was a nasty fall.

Three days of misery later, an attentive Vietnamese doctor made a house call to the hotel and recommended rehydration fluid immediately. He also told us to turn off the overhead fan because it was wicking away my body's ability to sweat out the fever. My fever broke within an hour.

Almost four months of constant companionship confirmed what drew me to Chris in the first place: he was grounded, kind, and patient. Travel can test you, and Chris aced it the entire way. His tireless care for me that week made him a minor celebrity with the hotel staff. As I recuperated in bed for the next four days, I envied the geckos scampering across the high ceiling. It seemed impossible I would ever regain my firm footing, let alone dart with such verve.

I arrived in Vietnam lean and strong, but my illness temporarily sapped my energy and decimated my appetite. My first morning upright, I shuffled a few blocks while clinging to Chris's arm for support, stopping to recover on a city bench. Slowly, I ate my way back to health. Fresh *bánh mì*, often paired with Laughing Cow soft cheese wedges, was a kind of medicine. Both were easy to digest and plentiful. These two items were the food equivalents of naturalized citizens. Introduced by the French generations earlier, they became fully integrated into the urban Vietnamese diet. I greeted them as long-lost friends after my eighteen months in China, where baguettes and cheese were as scarce as capitalists. My stomach was drawn to their comfort.

Over the next five weeks we traveled the spine of Vietnam by bus and boat and ended up in Saigon. Far from treating us as former aggressors, the Vietnamese we met were gracious and welcoming. This openness was disarming at first, then liberating when it proved to be genuine. At that time, the United States and Vietnam were putting the finishing touches on a trade agreement that would normalize diplomatic ties. Chris and I felt in a small way like an advance team. The Vietnamese eagerly accepted our dollars, and the country buzzed with infrastructure projects and the din of the thousands of motor scooters zigzagging the streets at all hours.

I booked a flight from Saigon to Philadelphia to spend Christmas with my family. Chris was flying to Seattle for the same reason. I landed on the East Coast a full day earlier than planned and took a train to my sister's college dorm room outside of the city. We drove across town to surprise my parents the next morning. It all worked beautifully. Their world traveler was home to rest.

In photos from that Christmas, I was still strikingly underweight. My collarbone looked like a choker and my cheekbones were sharp with definition. But my eyes shone with a solid self-assurance as my twenty-three-year-old body adjusted to its new lightness.

Tea

I hesitate to call myself a tea snob—but I am one. I will not turn down a packet of Lipton's Yellow Label if it is all that is on hand, yet I will judge every sip inferior.

I have come to have the utmost respect for the relational nature of tea. Tea alone does not make a meal, but I have sat down to many meals that would have been left wanting without it. Whether served at short breakfasts or dinners that dally into evening, tea is adept at launching a day or topping it off.

There is never a wrong moment for tea. News arrives of misfortune? Put the kettle on for comfort. Good news comes at last? Steep a mug and revel. Fever and chills? Turn to tea for its healing properties. Neighbors due for a barbecue? Iced tea, please.

Tea has distinct qualities from country to country, and its place in our psychic well-being is universal.

Teatime!

My stash of Tippy Orthodox Assam is one of the first items I pack whenever I travel. Given its crucial role in my morning ritual, I prefer its safe transport in my carry-on, though the container is often large enough to warrant the belly of a plane. I have become that person, the one who brings her own tea.

Hot. Strong. Milky. That is how I take my tea. I will gladly down a tall glass of iced tea when the thermometer's mercury creeps ever higher, but I always start the day with my customary hot beverage. Tea sets my morning in motion and often punctuates my afternoon. I pore over loose-leaf tea catalogs with the attention and longing of a gardener reading seed catalogs in winter.

My first consistent tea consumption took place in China. Ribbons of black and green tea leaves sank and swirled in ceramic mugs with matching lids to seal in the heat, steeping sometimes, by my lights, to a bitterness beyond drinkability. I became aware that tea was a necessary relational lubricant in China's social structure. This realization was made more complex by China's fiction of a classless society—it was in actuality one of stratified rank and power. At that time I was largely ignorant of tea as a product with influence (outside of the story of a band of colonists who launched a revolution by tossing chests of the stuff into Boston Harbor).

I associated Chinese bureaucracy with tea steeped in homemade glass jar thermoses to the point it resembled bog water—which is about how it tasted to me. I was drawn to the warmth yet found the astringency a killjoy. I could say as much for the China I encountered as a college student in 1991. They showed me true generosity of spirit, and yet the overbearing nature of the Chinese state left a foul taste in my mouth. This was less than two years after Chinese students defied orders and marched in Tiananmen Square, and college campuses around China still felt the aftershocks of the crackdown. At the same time China afforded me freedom to travel and challenge myself, it discouraged the same behavior in my Chinese peers.

Enter Michael and Leslie, who changed my tea habits and set me on my devotional path. Michael and I met when we were seven, and we attended high school together. We reconnected after college when Michael, now married to Leslie, moved to the Forestry College in Kunming to teach and do research. I was back in China visiting my parents, who were teaching in Beijing, and enthusiastically accepted Michael's invitation to visit. The plan was to stay two weeks. I ended up moving into an empty apartment next door and stayed for two months. Instead of leaving me feeling like a third wheel, Michael and Leslie were like two strong trees I could hang a hammock between and relax.

They introduced me to milky tea and the virtues of a midafternoon teatime, as well as prioritizing tea quality. I learned the difference between Assam and oolong, and that the nubbins of Gunpowder Green produced a cup tasting like the ocean. I loved how the sociable pause for tea bridged lunch and dinner, and how Leslie's liberal addition of milk made Chinese tea more palatable to me.

We bought milk from a traveling milkman who visited the neighborhood regularly with an aluminum jug lashed to his bike. The milk was often so fresh it was still warm. Customers gathered with lidded pots or containers for pints, which our milkman filled with a funnel, steady hands, and a sizeable spoon. Our tea (and homemade yogurt) addictions tested the volume limits of what customers could reasonably ask for without receiving murmured tut-tuts from the neighbors for being greedy.

The milky tea—and Michael and Leslie's company—reinforced my increasingly comfortable coexistence with China. Milk did not dull my tea; it calmed it and heightened its flavor. The milky tea that Leslie still prepares when I visit them now remains one of my best-loved preparations.

I marvel at the ubiquity of tea and its versatility when it comes to consumption and cultural norms. From Iceland to Argentina people convene over tea. I nursed bowls of salty yak-butter tea in the thin air of Lhasa and sipped thimblefuls of spiced, sweet tea next to apricot groves in northern Pakistan. In Turkey tulip-shaped glasses held rosy tea and sugar of a shade similar to the rooibos brew that I sipped with breakfast in Johannesburg. England introduced me to the cheerful pop of the kettle announcing a full boil and the gurgle of scalding water poured over round tea sachets.

We read the future in its leaves. We heal our bodies with its antioxidants. We still the mind with each swallow. Tea has been valued beyond gold, welcomed new friends, and soothed weary travelers.

Today, my tea steeps each morning in a cast-iron teapot Michael and Leslie gave me. Tea is foundational. I build my world every day on its constancy.

This is the year for you to go to the Rocky Horror Picture Show at the Varsity some Saturday night.

This is the year for you to climb the water tower at Volunteer Park and visit their greenhouse (better view than the space needle--and free!).

I moved to Seattle in 1994. Formerly a mossy backwater, the city was now a growing economic powerhouse. After sixteen months of eating through Asia, I joined the throngs of my peers migrating to the Pacific Northwest. Amtrak allowed shipment of up to five fifty-pound boxes with the purchase of a cross-country ticket, so I packed all of my belongings and clickity-clacked from Philadelphia to Seattle.

What first struck me about Seattle was how young it felt not only demographically but also architecturally. I grew up outside a city where some of the brownstones were over three hundred years old and many of the streets were designed for horse carriages. Seattle's wide streets and houses, by comparison, seemed to have been built the day before. I was most at home in older sections of Seattle, where the buildings, streetlamps, and storefronts had seen a modern city mushroom out of the wet environs.

I had swapped coasts and, in the process, swapped cultures. While many of the first Europeans settling the Northeast were desperate to flee the religious constraints of England, the first Europeans to settle the Pacific Northwest were a different breed from a later time. Their migration was propelled by a sense of discovery, the allure of financial gain (often pursued ruthlessly at the expense of native populations), and brazen entitlement. I saw a trailblazing attitude embodied in the ease and swagger of long-time residents who traced their family trees back to Seattle's muddy roots in 1851.

Seattle's murky skies cozied me, its love of books and film enchanted me, and the youthful energy motivated me. My first months turned into first years. I went from the liminal state of friendlessness to the point where I could brainstorm a guest list and throw a party. The party of choice was obvious: Chinese New Year.

This fusion of food and friends was about bridging my worlds. Seattle was now home, but parts of China still felt like home too. As did Philadelphia. And Maine. My Chinese New Year party was based in Seattle, but encapsulated my broader belief that home is who I am with as well as where I am.

Dumpling Party

AS A LUNAR CALENDAR HOLIDAY, Chinese New Year is a moving target, falling somewhere between mid-January and early February. The timing was excellent for a party in Seattle. Wintertime was dark and waterlogged, so diversions were welcome. Homemade dumplings fit the bill because their sociability matched mine. They were the ultimate meal of co-creation, allowing guests and hosts to blur into a gathering of eager eaters.

Everyone I could think of received an invitation. Old friends who resettled in the area. New friends from the Pacific Northwest. Friends from college. Friends from work. Friends from former jobs. Friends from graduate school. Friends of my roommates, John and Sylvia, which was only fair since I hijacked our house the day before the party, the day of the party, and then the day after for cleanup. If relatives were in town, they came. Neighbors. Friends of friends. The freedom of no limit to the guest list was part of the excitement of the party. The more the merrier. There would always be enough dumplings: no matter the size of your party, dumplings scale.

Because the party marked Chinese New Year, I wallpapered the downstairs with the Chinese character *fú* (福), which stands for fortune or good luck. Red paper lanterns made appearances, and I filled fruit bowls with satsuma oranges and placed them around the living room. I wrote fortunes that I tucked into small red envelopes adorned with gold characters. In keeping with the custom of exchanging money via red envelopes at high holidays, I included with each fortune three pennies. Three is an auspicious number in China. The fortunes all centered on Seattle and included very specific prognostications, such as "This is the year you will take the ferry to Bainbridge Island" or "This is the year you will attend the excellent book readings at Elliott Bay Book Company!"

The fortunes were really for me. Even though I sent each guest off with one, I wrote most with my own aspirations in mind, hoping that by sharing my wish lists, I might actually accomplish them myself. A few fortunes were written from my own experiences and my desire to share parts of the city and region I now called home. I liked hearing what people did with their fortunes and knowing that some looked forward all year to what would be divulged in their red envelopes. Friends told me that they tacked them to their bulletin boards, stuck them to their refrigerators, and used them as bookmarks to remind them that new experiences awaited in our collective backyard.

Dumpling preparations began with a checklist. Flour? Check. Pork? Check. Scallions? Check. Carrots and ginger? Check. Spinach and tofu? Check. Check. Soy sauce? Check. Vinegar? Check. Every year my preparation and proportions improved. I took notes after each party to tweak both the volume of ingredients and the steps to create the dough and fillings. I worked without formal recipes, following in the footsteps of the families in China who first introduced me to the deliciousness that occurs with the right mix of water, salt, and flour. Too much of one or the other and you end up with either Play-Doh or soup. In the early years, I asked visiting Chinese students to my house a week in advance for a refresher course in making the consummate dumpling.

This is how I like to cook in general: give me a list of ingredients and then let me experiment until I get a feel for the dish. Dumpling prep is forgiving. If the dough is too salty, put in more flour and water. Not enough pork in the filling? Heat some water, slice some more cabbage, and incorporate both into the mixture. Too much ginger? No such thing!

Dumplings can feed an empty stomach or an entire village. They can be steamed, boiled, or fried. In the case of my dumpling party, it was a four-burner operation for boiling, testing the limits of our kitchen stove. I put out a call for pots each year until my own collection of restaurant-issue vats was large enough to accommodate the volume that upwards of seventy hungry mouths required.

The dining room table hosted the assembly line: floured hands rolled tacky dough into long "snakes," then carefully cleavered them into lumps and pressed them into thin coaster-sized disks to be filled. Conversation mingled with the whackety-whack of knives and the thunk of rolling pins as hands gently cupped dumplings to be stuffed and pinched closed for boiling.

I spent the party engaged in a game of Concentration personified, connecting guests from different orbits with common interests. Between bites of dumpling, I surveyed the room for possible pairings. I pulsed like a firefly when I saw friends who were unknown to one another an hour earlier deep in conversation or laughing. A benefit of collecting my growing galaxy of friends under one roof was that it expanded everyone's community. Along with choreographing meetings between strangers, I encouraged my guests to eat their fill, insisting that one always had room for one more dumpling.

The dining room and kitchen teemed. Periodically, I checked in on the dumpling makers and whisked baking sheets with rows of dumplings to the boiling water. My friends on stove duty watched dumplings bob to the surface as they cooked, ready to scoop them out with a strainer and transfer them to serving bowls where they would be dipped in chili-spiked vinegar and soy sauce and gobbled up in no time. This life cycle of a dumpling went on for hours.

The party suited a range of personalities: the social butterflies worked the room, and those who preferred to avoid small talk had tasks that gave them a vital role. Almost everyone took at least one stint at the dining room table, and some enthusiasts stayed there for hours, falling into a meditative state of dumplingness. Practice paid off and dumplings were built with greater dexterity. Rookie mistakes included overfilling, which left the poor dumpling too compromised to withstand the rapids of boiling water. If the ratio of dough to filling favored the dough too much, a dumpling could lack that splendid taste explosion.

The kitchen windows steamed up with the stove's exertions, and I kept cool drinks filled for my friends who faithfully oversaw the boiling. When the heat grew to be too much, we threw open the back door and Seattle's cold air rushed in. Friends spilled out onto the sagging porch to continue chatting, plates of dumplings in hand.

I hold fast to the memory of so many friends together in one place. My first years in Seattle had me feeling like a modern homesteader—a transplant ticking off years until the land was truly mine. But time and land alone do not a community make. Friends in my house those nights made Seattle my home.

The news of East and West Germans splintering the Berlin Wall with pickaxes in 1989 became tangible when a college friend brought me back a hand-sized chunk of the wall from his visit to Berlin. One side was painted the purple color iridescent gasoline creates on water. After hearing the breathless radio broadcasts from the city and watching the widespread rejoicing that followed, I held history in my hand. The wall was notorious for its durability, and there were many stories of the inventive ways people attempted to cross the border undetected. One of my favorites was about a woman smuggled out between two hollowed-out surfboards.

My first trip to Berlin was much less covert, though I do love a surprise arrival.

Thanksgiving in Berlin

I RARELY TRAVELED at Thanksgiving. Jockeying with millions of other travelers held no appeal, nor did sky-high travel costs. But in 2001, Berlin was irresistible. Reservations plummeted after September 11, and airlines responded by slashing prices. I could fly from Seattle to Berlin for less than it would cost to fly home to Philadelphia. Yet it was the people I would see in Germany who tipped the scales.

The idea was to spend the holiday with three German friends—Ansgar, Markus, and Johannes—who had been exchange students on graduate fellowships at the University of Washington the year before. We had bonded over a shared fascination with politics and a love of the television show *The West Wing*. We piled into my living room many a Wednesday night to watch the show, following the rapid-fire dialog that most native English speakers found challenging to track. Talking politics with peers from outside the United States who were also political science students well versed in our political system was enlightening. That year, I played the role of beaming older sister to her dashing and beloved younger brothers from Europe.

That academic year flew by, and by the time Thanksgiving rolled around, they had all returned to their respective schools, so I had not seen any of them for a number of months. It was a flipped script: an American packing her family recipes to prepare a Thanksgiving meal in a country that did not observe the holiday. On top of that, my arrival was a surprise for Ansgar, schemed in e-mails with Adam. Adam had been an exchange student that same year and would fly from his native London to join us in Berlin. We were giddy from plotting our friendly subterfuge.

The plan unfolded without a hitch. Ansgar's flat in the Berlin neighborhood of Kreuzberg brought grandeur to our Thanksgiving meal. Though the kitchen was compact, high ceilings accentuated a large, sumptuous main room with windows overlooking the tree-lined street. Happy ghosts from Berlin's golden age in the 1920s glided approvingly from room to room. In any other city, the flat would have been beyond the reach of graduate students, but Berlin was still fighting its way back to economic health.

Many friends were invited in the spirit of a Thanksgiving table that can always fit one more. We spent much of Thanksgiving morning navigating wintry Berlin, food shopping for potatoes, butter, cream, pumpkin, and other fixings on our list. The city that had been severed was now almost twelve years reunified. My friends were boys at the time of reunification; now half their lives had been lived in an era of integration and new national identity. Sleek trams hummed down thoroughfares, linking former East and West neighborhoods. To my untrained eyes, the old divide between Berlin's halves was invisible. The city felt whole, not merely reconnected. Our expedition was complete when we found a turkey that would fit in Ansgar's shoebox of an oven. Home we went, and the kitchen commotion began.

I was air traffic control, put in charge of divvying up tasks because of my previous Thanksgiving experience. Potatoes were boiled and mashed. The turkey was seasoned, baked, and basted. Cheeses were unwrapped and arranged. Wines were uncorked to breathe. Side dishes seemed to appear out of thin air—as did a few pies.

A blanket-as-tablecloth covered the floor of the main room, turning this Thanksgiving into a picnic. Plates were filled, then filled again. Some guests sported snappy vests and ties, fitted wool skirts, or cashmere sweaters—I was charmed by their sartorial finery. Johannes queued up a playlist after dessert, and the blanket morphed into a dance floor. Our bodies fizzed to the music for hours.

I went to Berlin anticipating a lavish Thanksgiving, never expecting to find equal bounty over breakfast. I woke up each morning and made my way into the kitchen to find an array of breads, jams, eggs, sliced cheeses, meats, yogurt, applesauce, and baked goods. The teapot whistled. Hot coffee perked. I know these morning meals were likely embellished for my benefit. I do the same when hosting by flipping pancakes, folding omelets, and baking muffins with the best of them. However, those mornings in Germany drove home that a breakfast banquet only requires a stocked fridge and maybe a quick visit to a local baker for fresh bread. This was a meal of abundance you could sit down to daily.

There were many moments in Berlin where I wanted to bottle time. Seattle had been a catapult for all of my friends, and they were on exciting career trajectories. During that Thanksgiving in Berlin, though, I still played the pace car, taking one more lap before releasing the field. We ate, then accelerated forward, delighted by our speed.

I trace my love of road trips back to the annual vacations my family took to Wisconsin nearly every summer of my childhood. While much of my travel since has involved passports and planes, neither was required for these early cross-country treks.

I appreciate the miles that roll by beyond a car window differently than the ones at thirty thousand feet. Plane travel challenges my bearings—I wake up in Amsterdam and bunk down in my Seattle bed. Though I am grateful for the speed of reentry, I also have to manage its consequences as I slide between worlds, even familiar ones.

The long days driving to and from Wisconsin were worth it for the weeks spent swimming in Lost Land Lake. The family cabin was less than ten feet from the shore. Our dock jutted out from the lakefront to form a large T, its planks sun-scorched by the height of the day. The water was more green than blue, and the light cast sunbeams below the surface. Our rhythms decelerated as we sank into life in the woods and water. Days stretched and had seasons unto themselves: chilly mornings gave way to hot afternoons that cooled again for bedtime.

North Woods

GROWING UP, I had a streak of twelve straight summer vacations in the North Woods, as many refer to upstate Wisconsin. Lakes glittered with splashes of white birch on the banks, so inviting that I hardly changed out of my swimsuit. Fuzzy young ferns under my bare feet made shoes optional. Our cabin sat at the end of a long unpaved driveway that formed a large circle at the end. Many a summer when our trusty Valiant crept toward the last five hundred feet of a two- or three-day marathon drive, my parents would let my sister and me hop out to walk the final leg. We burst into the main cabin like long-lost explorers.

My extended family congregated for supper around a long rectangular yellow Formica kitchen island with small vases of Queen Anne's lace or clover picked from the surrounding woods by one of us children and presented triumphantly to an adult. My paternal grandfather did the bulk of the cooking. As our clan grew, meal prep began to rotate. Yet when I think of that kitchen stove, I always see Grandpa John at it, spatula in hand, apron on, whistling.

I watched him chop, mince, toss, stir, roast, and fry with efficiency. He seamlessly produced meals for a dozen, and if he used a recipe, I never saw it. His ability to prep, maneuver between many burners and the oven at once, and then present a finished meal was that of a virtuoso. He used large, wide-bottomed pans and tossed ingredients while applying heat. Spices and salt were added by feel and taste. He took the basics—meat, pasta, vegetables—and artfully turned them into meals for many. The setting sun bathed suppers in a honeyed glow as the light bounced off the water and onto the wood-paneled cabin walls.

That last meal of the day we all ate together, but breakfasts were staggered, given everyone's particular morning regimen. My grandparents were the earliest birds. Each night before heading to bed, my grandmother, Mary-Blanche, arranged their breakfast place settings at the end of the kitchen island. Two juice glasses stenciled with oranges waited overnight alongside expectant cutlery, napkins, plates, and bowls. It felt special to witness this evening tradition and the practice of anticipating the first meal of the day. The intentionality also bespoke the adoration my grandparents had for one another. The ceremonial aspect diverged from my grab-and-dash bowl of breakfast cereal. Their ritual had a touch of formality that I interpreted as a quaint feature of my grandparents' generation, like the cotton nightcaps they wore to bed. By the time I sat down to breakfast, their dishes were cleared and a fire roared in the river-rock fireplace, taking the nip off the cool Wisconsin mornings.

My family sold the cabin more than a decade ago, after Grandpa John and Grandma M-B died. It has been years since I have bitten into the summer-sweet kernels of freshly shucked and boiled Wisconsin corn, smelled a coil of punk lit to drive away ravenous mosquitoes, or felt the chalky softness of birch bark. But every night I ready my own kitchen before bedtime and put out my breakfast items as a nod to my grandparents' preparations for shared tomorrows.

Creamery Fresh

HEAVY CREAM

DAILY........PER. QT.

2000 Gals
of
America's Freshest. Finest
MILK ON HAND

CHOICE
NATURAL

WEDRICL. MAPLE SYRUP

I have twice delivered humanitarian communications trainings for GOAL, an international development organization. GOAL, head-quartered in Ireland, has offices on four continents. The program works to alleviate humanitarian crises with basic-needs interven-tion programs. In 2015, the GOAL Syria office was one of their largest operations. Humanitarian communications refers to the ethical documentation of programs that provide food, water, and shelter. Photos, video, and audio all can contribute to the story-telling process.

My host at GOAL Syria assured me that I would be amazed by the dedication of the GOAL Syria staff. She also assured me I would eat well. She was right on both counts.

Breakfast in Syria

THE LIVELY CITY of Antakya is nestled in a valley formed by the Nur Mountains, fourteen miles from the Mediterranean Sea in Turkey's southernmost tip. As my plane shuddered through the updrafts to its safe landing at the airport, I distracted myself by craning my neck to peer out the window at the green farmland below. It was hard to believe that Syria, just twelve miles away, was a war zone. The scale of that human suffering was also hard to fathom. By the time I arrived, the war had displaced almost eight million Syrians internally and sent another three million seeking refuge outside the country.

It took all of three days in Turkey to fall head over heels for Istanbul, my point of entry. My friend Vicki, the GOAL Syria country director, flew up from Antakya to join me, and we spent hours catching up over meals. Breakfasts included *simit*, rings of chewy bread covered with sesame seeds; strands of salty cheese; fresh yogurt with sliced fruit; local honey; and strong coffee. Seeing the city by foot and ferry built appetites for midday and evening meals that included treacly grilled plum and meatball kebobs; crispy zucchini and leek

Svenka
ANTAKYA
MARCH · 25 · 2015

PEYNIRLI BÖREK
börek w/ local cheese

FLAT BREAD

KAZ BAŞI
LOKUM
tenderloin cubes w/ baked mushrooms

VIŞNELI KEBAP
meat balls in cherry sauce
pita slices

SUCUK ROLL
cylinders of spicy meat paste on pita

mint sprigs, peppers, and lime wedges

FETTUŞ
lettuce, cucumber, tomato, sumac vinaigrette, pita, cheese, pomegranate syrup

SÜZME YOĞURT
strained yogurt

walnut paste with red peppers
MUHAMMARA

H₂O

ALİ NAZİK
yogurt with roasted eggplant and meat cubes

HUMUS
mashed chickpea with tahini, lemon juice, garlic paste and olive oil.

@avardt3 2015

patties; baked artichoke hearts topped with carrots; green salad with mint; *muhammara*, a dip made by grinding red peppers, walnuts, and pomegranates; and sweet semolina cake topped with fruit puree and homemade cream. Courses were accompanied by bottles of nose-tickling carbonated water, followed by tea served in glass teacups often stenciled with gold-leaf trim. Good food and friends did wonders for jet lag, and then it was time to get down to work.

For safety reasons, GOAL Syria operated out of Turkey. The plan was to have all GOAL staff working on the ground in Syria join my humanitarian communications training in Turkey. However, the Turkish government closed the border a week before my arrival, so more than half of the participants had no choice but to use an online platform in an environment with tenuous Internet connectivity. To make matters worse, two of the cities where most of the Syrian-based participants lived were bombed the night of our first day of training.

One participant, Waleed, was determined to use the online platform and follow along with the training, regularly typing thoughtful comments and questions in the chat box. On the second day of the training, the on-site participants did an outdoor photo shoot to tell a story in three photographs. The chat box lit up with a question from Waleed.

"How can I complete this assignment, Anita? It is not safe to go outdoors."

I thought fast and typed faster.

"Waleed, you do not have to go outside to tell a story. I bet there is a story you can photograph inside your home."

He answered right back.

"My wife is making breakfast. Do you mean I could tell a story about that?"

I pounded out my response.

"Yes!"

As Waleed considered how to compose his three photographs of a family breakfast, I remembered my breakfast in Antakya the day before with Vicki and another GOAL colleague. The café was set above the central roundabout in Antakya, with panoramic views of the mountains that enfolded the city. Our table was crowded with matching white dishes: a puddle of honey sprinkled with walnuts and three islands of *kaymak*, Turkish clotted cream; sliced cucumber; wrinkled black olives and smooth green ones; sliced tomatoes; a tangle of string cheese; dried apricots; yogurt dusted with sumac powder and olive oil; *tahin pekmez*, made of dried tahini and molasses; and a basket of warm pita bread triangles. As I was trying to decide what to eat first, a small metal pan appeared with fried eggs. I decided then and there that I could live in Turkey for their breakfasts alone.

Now my thoughts shifted from the relative safety and comfort of that breakfast to the vulnerability of Waleed's.

Humanitarian agencies are often thought of as being in the business of providing things—tents, water, blankets, food. However, giving life to stories is important, and they deserve to be shared with the wider world. War zones, disease outbreaks, and natural disasters can turn people into abstractions and statistics. Humanitarian communications mindfully documents stories that show resilience, optimism, and staggering perseverance despite unspeakable sorrow and horror. Perhaps most importantly, telling stories in a way that preserves the dignity of those involved reminds us all of what we have in common—such as the fact that life continues amidst upheaval. You get up in the morning and make breakfast for those you love.

When people face extreme circumstances, meals and the mundane assume added significance. What we eat and whom we eat it with define who we are: our tastes and our kinship ties. In the case of Waleed that morning, breakfast could also be seen as an act of resolve. You can bomb my city, but I will still start my day drinking tea and eating bread with my wife and two sons.

Relief agencies are well positioned to bear witness to conflict and resolution. The stories they hear at a grassroots level become part of the country's collective memory. Some of those memories are snapshots of unbearable loss and, in the case of Syria, a crushing sense of abandonment by the international community. However, other memories are offered by organizations like GOAL, which, in the face of persistent roadblocks and great personal risk, did not leave Syrians to suffer alone.

Waleed e-mailed me his three-photo story that evening. I clicked open the three attachments one by one, watching each pixelated line appear to form a complete image on my laptop screen.

In a war zone, setting out breakfast at home with your family is more than just an act of love—it is hope. That is always a story worth telling.

ACKNOWLEDGMENTS

To everyone who has ever shared a meal with me, thank you. You are a part of this book.

A symphony of thanks to Chin Music Press. My publisher Bruce Rutledge has a commitment to the art of bookmaking that quickens my pulse with happiness. When my book was still just a brainstorm, former Chin Music publicist Chelsey Slattum provided welcome encouragement, and then provided vision when she returned to the project on special assignment leading up to its publication. Chin Music editor Allie Draper possessed eagle eyes for the smallest details as well as the larger narrative patterns. She polished the book to a shine. Cali Kopczick gave key editing support in the home stretch. Guidance from Chin Music publicist Maddy Burton has made tooting my own horn fun. Olenka Burgess delivered a social media strategy that was second to none. Author Kate Lebo blazed the trail for me at Chin Music with her genre-busting book, *A Commonplace Book of Pie*, for which I am grateful.

Dan Shafer has a sixth sense for taking ramblings over many cups of coffee and transforming them into exactly the aesthetic imagined. His listening skills are reflected in his excellent graphic design work. Dan had wonderful images to work with, thanks in large part to Josh Samson, who hosted us in his studio for a full-day photography shoot that was a perfect example of collaboration and the creative process.

I am fortunate to call many talented writers friends. Hsiao-Ching Chou and Cheryl Sternman Rule looked at early drafts that showed promise but little else and buoyed my spirits to stick with it. Kristy Leissle, Rachel Gold, and Leslie Walker Williams wielded their mighty pens on later drafts, immeasurably improving the manuscript. The only two pages of my book that have not been brilliantly edited by Jessica Esch—umpteen times—are these.

The University of Washington has been my professional playground for twenty years. Joyful thanks to the Department of Communication and to my Communication Leadership graduate program community. Storytelling is central to our work; thank you for motivating me to tell mine. Thanks also to the Department of Global Health for colleagues and travel that proved to be rich material for my book.

Friends make everything better, including this book. Everyone I asked granted me permission to use their names in the essays. My profound appreciation to each of you. A trusted group joined my manuscript-minders and when surveyed told me to go back to the drawing board on the subtitle, so I did. This nudge made the difference. Special thanks to Naomi Ishisaka, who hired me for my first food writing gig. She banked on my enthusiasm mitigating my inexperience.

My parents, Betsy and Dan Crofts, raised my sister Sarah and me to take on the world and taught us that it would in turn take us in. They were right and then some. The hearth and home they gave us allows me to recreate it wherever I am. My love for these three is limitless.

And lastly extra thanks to Jess for always keeping my corners cornered.

A.V. CROFTS has been published in *Gastronomica, Saveur, Arcade, ColorsNW,* and the four-volume set, *Food Cultures of the World Encyclopedia.* She teaches at the University of Washington Communication Leadership graduate program and is on faculty at the Department of Communication and the Department of Global Health. She lives in Seattle and Maine.

Visit www.pepperforthebeast.com to see where she's eating next.

COLOPHON

THIS BOOK IS SET in Mercury Text and Akzidenz Grotesque with scattered accents of a custom brush lettering. It was designed by Dan D Shafer in Seattle, Washington in the spring and early summer of 2016. The text pages are printed on 80# Rolland Opaque. Printing and binding were expertly handled by Marquis in Montreal, Quebec.